DAWSON COAL
HYDRO-CLEANED

COAL TOWN

COAL TOWN

THE LIFE AND TIMES OF
DAWSON, NEW MEXICO

Toby Smith

ANCIENT CITY PRESS
SANTA FE, NEW MEXICO

International Standard Book Number
0-941270-81-5

Book design by Mary Powell

Cover photograph: Last coal car dumped, April 28, 1950.

Frontispiece: Dawson's tree-lined main street.

Smith, Toby, 1946-
    Coal town : the life and times of Dawson, New Mexico / by Toby Smith.
        p.   cm.
    Includes bibligraphical references (p. 131).
    ISBN 0-941270-81-5.—ISBN 0-941270-82-3 (pbk.)
    1. Dawson (N.M.)—History. 2. Coal mines and mining—New Mexico—
Dawson—History. I. Title.
F804.D39S65 1994   93-43245
978.9'22—dc20   CIP

10 9 8 7 6 5 4 3 2

for Dawsonites everywhere

"Oh, that's the town I knew as a little girl. And, look, there's the old white fence that used to be around our house. Oh, I'd forgotten that! Oh, I love it so!"

—Thornton Wilder, *Our Town*

CONTENTS

PREFACE

Whatever you do, don't call Dawson a ghost town.

Granted, no one resides today in the place where 6,000 people each night used to lay down their heads. Fewer than a half-dozen buildings now stand in an area that once sprouted nearly 500. And Dawson has vanished—been erased is the only way to put it—from most New Mexico road maps and atlases. But don't call it a ghost town, at least not to a Dawsonite. I made that mistake—once.

Early in the course of researching this book, I rather smugly mentioned something like, "It's too bad that Dawson's a ghost town." The former Dawson resident to whom I made the remark suddenly scrutinized me over the top of her spectacles. "Young man," she said, in a voice that suggested I surely couldn't find my way home at night, "the town's plenty alive."

Sadly, numerous people simply don't recognize the living nature of Dawson. Once so forward-looking, the town, located approximately thirty-six miles southwest of Raton, for several years has existed only in the memories of too many people: *That's where all the coal miners died, isn't it?* Admittedly, the name regularly appears in *The World Almanac* under the heading "Principal U.S. Mine Disasters." Dawson, in fact, is included twice in the yearly reference source. More men were killed in Dawson's mine explosions than at the Battle of Little Bighorn, though Custer's Last Stand is far better known.

Aside from the mining disasters and the structure of the local government, which was controlled by the owning company, Dawson was much like any other thriving small town. Then why do hundreds of people think it so special? Dawson was, as those who spent time there are wont to say, a way of life. It grew from a tent city to a town of thirty square miles, the largest town in the Southwest supported by a single industry. Dawson was a busy place, certainly—from 1899 until 1950, the town's mines produced more than 33 million saleable tons of coal, a fact that adds to its singularity. Moreover, a dozen different languages were spoken in Dawson, making it "an early United Nations," as one resident described it.

But Dawson's uniqueness derives from more than its background or its underground. Often memories have a way of becoming more agreeable as time passes, and what seemed harsh sixty years ago now frequently seems wonderful. That is true concerning memories of Dawson—to a point. Dawson wasn't an idyllic spot; nobody has ever claimed as much. Rather, it was a peerless place in terms of being different. Like delegates to the United Nations, members of the community got along. When novelist and historian Wallace Stegner theorized, "Cooperation mattered more than self-reliance in the rugged West," he could have been speaking of Dawson. People—of almost every race and color, of almost every ethnic and religious persuasion—came together in Dawson and, in work and in play, usually did so harmoniously. Five decades after the town closed, that common denominator of amicability still exists in the hearts of anyone with a link to the place. Not a ghost town, Dawson is a *real* town that continues to inspire a fidelity that exceeds nearly any *alma mater*.

I came into this world as Dawson was departing it, but I have had the opportunity, since embarking on this project, to explore the physical remains of the town several times, in all four seasons, in fact. Those visits have helped me, in part, to understand Dawson's endurance. I've been there in the fall, when the junipers and piñons fill the canyons with a paradisal scent. I've stopped by in the winter, when the mesas, lightly crowned with snow, resemble wedding cakes. In the spring, I've watched the wind bend the scrub grass at the feet of the cemetery's iron crosses. And, during a Dawson Picnic, among the ruins of a once proud place, I've felt the warmth of the summer sun on my back and heard the laughter of people who were glad, once more, to be home.

I had the pleasure of interviewing more than 100 people for this book, and it was through their still strong emotional attachments that I truly learned why Dawson continues to be alive, to breathe. "When I close my eyes," one ex-inhabitant told me, "I can still see Dawson." Said another: "I was just plain lucky I was born there." A half dozen of the people I talked to were more than 90 years of age, and one had seen 100. Does being from Dawson generate longevity? Well, surely a fond recollection can be life's elixir.

I grew up in a small town 2,500 miles from Dawson. It was a nice enough community, with good schools, little crime, and plenty to do, much like Dawson. But in other ways the two places were not alike: lately, whenever I catch myself reflecting on my hometown, I realize it did not have Dawson's singular spirit of togetherness, its genuine warmth and friendliness that ex-residents simply won't let go of, won't let die and become a ghost town.

Perhaps the biggest compliment I can make is that, given a choice, I would like to have grown up in Dawson.

Toby Smith
Albuquerque

ACKNOWLEDGMENTS

Just as Dawson was and is special, this book could not have been born without the help of some special people. Carol McClary Myers stands—rather modestly, I might add—at the head of a line of midwives. I have long had the distinct feeling that if I were to take a straight pin and prick the tip of Carol's finger—with her permission, of course—the blood that would ooze out surely would be colored red *and* black, Dawson colors. Born and reared in Dawson, Carol, like so many others, would go live there in an instant, if she could. Carol guided this work from the very first. She quietly prodded me while at the same time gently explained the town to me, but never once did she explain it *down* to me. She deciphered my scribblings and retyped them and, whenever I got discouraged, reminded me repeatedly that a permanent written record of Dawson deserved a place in this world. Thanks, Carol.

Carol's husband, Dwight, though a Dawsonite only by marriage, feels just as connected to the town as any outsider can. Dwight is a bookman, and he felt this was one book long overdue. His advice on literary matters is equally appreciated.

For more times than I think she'd care to remember, I pestered Alberta McClary with telephone calls and questions about Dawson, and she, too, deserves singling out, for never once did Alberta complain about my inquiries, even when I asked the same question more than once.

Robert McClary, with whom I tramped about Dawson one fine spring day, poking through the weeds and clambering over rocks and mentally making a map of the place, also rates a large debt of gratitude.

Anna and Bob Lucero, Marcia and George Beall, and the Scanlon brothers—Gene, Jerry, Roger, and Jim—supported this history, particularly in the early stages of labor when it needed more reinforcement than I could supply.

To David Holtby, who first put me on Dawson's trail, to Ann Mason, who tidied up that trail, and to Mary Powell, who kept the trail well-lighted, I am much obliged.

Like so many other Dawsonites, Nick Di Domenico holds his memories, even the not-so-happy ones, dear. Nick was the first to offer *all* his remembrances—as well as all his lunch— to me in Dawson. In the many months since meeting in the town, Nick, a trove of Dawsoniana, always has been quick to share any piece of it.

My wife, Susan, and our two sons, Jed and Kit, have heard more about Dawson in the last couple of years than they ever imagined they might. Amazingly, they never protested, and on several occasions wanted to know more. Their patience does not go unrecognized.

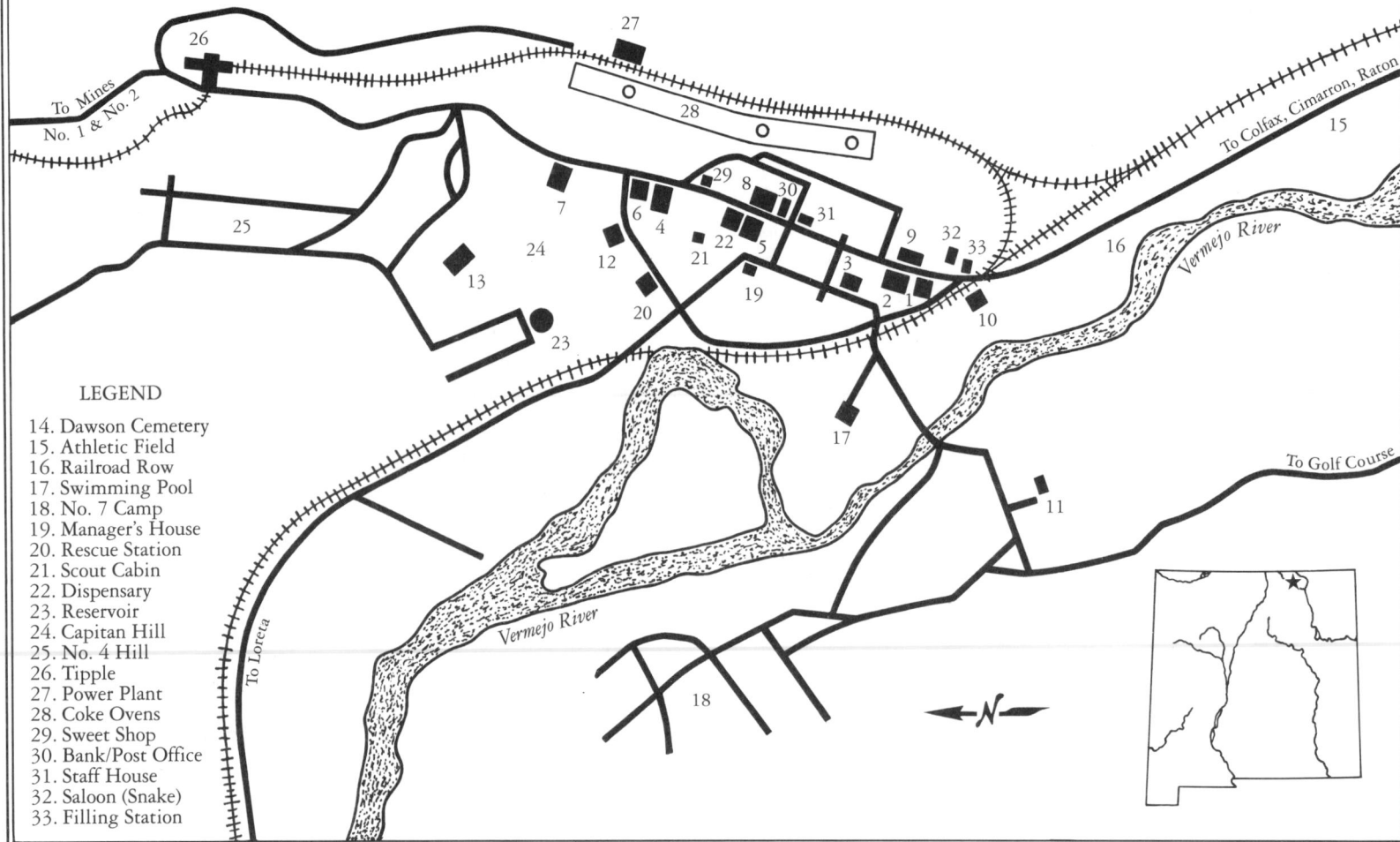

DAWSON, NEW MEXICO
CIRCA 1936

International Surveying & Mapping Company
Eureka, California
Compiled by Bob McClary

To Mines
No. 1 & No. 2

To Colfax, Cimarron, Raton

Vermejo River

15

16

Vermejo River

To Golf Course

To Loreta

Vermejo River

LEGEND

14. Dawson Cemetery
15. Athletic Field
16. Railroad Row
17. Swimming Pool
18. No. 7 Camp
19. Manager's House
20. Rescue Station
21. Scout Cabin
22. Dispensary
23. Reservoir
24. Capitan Hill
25. No. 4 Hill
26. Tipple
27. Power Plant
28. Coke Ovens
29. Sweet Shop
30. Bank/Post Office
31. Staff House
32. Saloon (Snake)
33. Filling Station

N

1. Gymnasium

2. Phelps Dodge Mercantile

3. Central School

4. Opera House

5. Hospital and Dispensary

6. Teacherage

7. Catholic Church

8. Main Office

9. Hotel

10. Depot

11. Ranch House

12. Community Church

13. Douglas School

Significant buildings are identified by number on facing page.

Reade

Chapter One

BEGINNING

*"He'd always lived where he
couldn't hear a train whistle."*

—Delphine Dawson Wilson

The stranger who appeared at the door of John Barkley Dawson's stately ranch house on the Vermejo River that day in the late 1880s had some bad news. He was a "grant man," meaning he represented the Maxwell Land Grant Company, owner of a sprawling mass of ground that blanketed northeastern New Mexico and reached into Colorado. Dawson always enjoyed visitors, though this one, after a minute or so, drawled, "You'll have to get off your property."

There was a time when Dawson, or J. B. as people called him, would have greeted such words with a six-shooter. A broad-beamed man with a well-trimmed Vandyke beard, Dawson had saddled up with the Texas Rangers and he'd shot down his share of Indians. He took guff from no one. But J. B. Dawson was also smart enough to know that hot words led to cold slabs. He hadn't become a successful businessman by getting violent, which a lot of people were doing in the Territory over this good-for-nothing land grant business. Homesteaders getting killed and vigilante groups running wild and blood being shed—all because some fancy-suited fellers didn't think a settler had rights to what was his free and clear.

Dawson had experienced enough turmoil in the last few years without worrying about whether he owned his land, which he knew he did. His first two wives had died in child-

John Barkley Dawson, 1830–1918:
his land became the town.

birth. Within a single year, three of his young sons were gone, too, one from measles, one from a ruptured appendix, and one as a result of being run over by a wagon. Yet another son had had his hand torn off in a roping accident. Those kinds of hardships had taught Dawson how to endure, and that was especially important now when somebody was standing at his door and ordering him to pack up and leave a place where he had lived for more than twenty years.

As he did all his guests, Dawson invited the grant man inside and fed him as he would anybody who came by the ranch, treating him to a meal of his own prized beef and fresh vegetables and pie, made from apples from his own giant orchard. Then, when the man had settled back with a pipe, J. B. announced matter-of-factly that nobody was going to push him from his home, from this stretch of bunch-grass and low bluffs and juniper and piñon that he had first seen in the early 1860s and selected because, well, out here in this lonesome but peaceful valley he'd never have to hear the sound of a train whistle.

John Barkley Dawson was not really a recluse, however. Family was important to him, and he had always wanted his kin around, from the time he was a boy in Kentucky, where he was born in Grayson County, on November 10, 1830. A distant relative of the American statesman and presidential candidate Henry Clay, Dawson, at age six, moved with his parents to a spread on the Arkansas River. He might have stayed there with them and farmed quietly all his life if he hadn't had a a hankering to see the West. In 1853, sturdily handsome and almost six feet tall, Dawson, accompanied by his mother and father, drove a team of oxen to California, in search of gold. Two years later, he moved more than 1,000 head of cattle from Arkansas to California, an extraordinary feat at the time. In California, he sold the stock to miners and then, still itching for adventure, sailed home. On his return through Panama, Dawson got in a knife fight with bandits who tried to rob him, and he suffered a gash to the leg. No sooner had he arrived back home when he moved his family to Texas, where, in 1858, he became a partner with the celebrated Charles Goodnight in a cattle outfit. For the next few years Dawson trailed herds from Texas to Colorado, becoming the first man to make the trip. During one such journey in 1861, Indians attacked and fired an arrow that tore through the center of Dawson's hand. As if he hadn't had enough adventure by now, he served intermittently with the Texas Rangers from 1864 to 1867, where he learned to love his enemies but keep his Winchester oiled.

While making a cattle drive in the 1860s, Dawson passed through the northern part of New Mexico Territory. There, he became particularly attracted to the *rincón* of the Vermejo River. Utes and Apaches could still be seen there, as could deer and wild turkey. Dawson was taken by the abundant bluestem and grama grass, where he knew stock could graze well. He liked how the canyons shielded the valley from wind and snow, and yet offered forage and spring water. Though the area was at 6,600 feet, the climate, Dawson noticed, seemed reasonably comfortable.

So impressed was he with the country that, on January 17, 1869, Dawson purchased a tract of land there from his friend Lucien Maxwell. At the time, Maxwell held the largest single piece of real estate in the United States ever owned by one person—almost 2 million acres. Because his part of Maxwell's grant was shaped rather like a glove, Dawson called it the "hand of God." A curiously worded deed described the piece as being "in the valley or draining of the Vermejo River . . .

beginning at a certain dam, at the head of a certain ditch, at the right-hand point of rocks, from thence running down the north side of said river to a certain other pile of rocks . . ." The land was believed to total 3,700 acres, and Dawson paid $1,000 for it.

The Maxwell Land Grant had originated in 1841 when Carlos Beaubien and Guadalupe Miranda were given a large tract east of Red River, by the Mexican government. Beaubien later purchased Miranda's interest. Maxwell, an affable fur trapper who came to the Territory on the advice of Kit Carson, married Beaubien's daughter and in time bought out the Beaubien heirs. Maxwell settled all claims on the property, some of which went back to the sixteenth century, though boundaries still remained uncertain. But Maxwell, like Dawson, was a searching sort and, instead of taking care of his holdings, began to speculate in gold on his land. To support this interest, Maxwell sold off pieces of his grant, one strangely shaped and peculiarly defined piece to J. B. Dawson. Another, a far larger chunk, went to a corporation of English speculators in 1870.

The speculators became the Maxwell Land Grant and Railway Company. But, because the boundaries of the grant were still questionable, the company had trouble selling the land and went bankrupt in 1875. Reorganized in 1880 as the Maxwell Land Grant Company, this group began to study who lived where on the grant, of particular interest since the railroad's arrival had made coal properties in the area, estimated at $1 billion, to be of prime importance. Agreements that residents had made with Lucien Maxwell suddenly were called worthless, and ejection lawsuits were initiated against alleged squatters. In retaliation, range wars broke out across northeastern New Mexico. The new owners received a vote of con-

J. B. Dawson's ranch house became a community landmark.

fidence in 1887 when the United States Supreme Court recognized the Maxwell Land Grant Company as the legal titleholder to the vast expanse.

While these maneuverings were going on, J. B. Dawson was settling in on the land he loved, thirty-six miles southwest of Raton. He had moved to his "hand of God" an extended family that included children, grandchildren, and even his parents. The Dawson clan lived in a large, adobe ranch house, a mansion of two stories and twelve rooms, with three-foot-thick walls. Dawson had by now added other portions of land to his Vermejo tract. Several hundred head of cattle grazed his land, along with 100 horses, and he had joined in partnership with stock companies in the region. He also had a vast orchard with more than forty-five varieties of apples. Dawson's reputation ran deep: he served as president of the Citizens National Bank of Raton, hunted bear with Territorial governors, and threw elaborate parties for friends and neighbors. A local newspaper praised him as "pioneer farmer, orchardist and stock raiser."

Dawson might also have been termed "coal miner." Though coal had been discovered in Raton as far back as 1820, nobody had done much about removing it, wood being the fuel of choice. But J. B., weary of splitting logs for his stoves, one day tried to ignite some of the coal he had scraped from a nearby mesa. The stuff burned so well that Dawson began to sell it to his neighbors.

When the Maxwell Land Grant Company learned how much coal lay in Dawson's backyard and that Dawson already was making money off it, company officials decided that they'd take Dawson to court and show him that his cocka-mamie deed from Lucien Maxwell was not worth the paper on which it was printed.

For his attorney, Dawson chose Andreius A. Jones of Las Vegas, who later became the first United States Senator from New Mexico after New Mexico entered statehood in 1912. A former schoolteacher in his late twenties, Jones convinced a San Miguel County district jury in 1891, and then the Territorial Supreme Court, that Dawson's deed was legitimate and that Maxwell, who had died in Fort Sumner, New Mexico, in 1875, made a lot of transactions in a language that could confound the most diligent surveyor.

In early 1894, *Maxwell Land Grant Company, Plaintiff in Error v. John B. Dawson*, reached the United States Supreme Court. The Court found that Dawson did not own 3,700 acres, as believed, but more than 20,000. However, the Court also found Dawson's deed baffling. Justice Henry Brown remarked: "It is incredible that any man should have paid

$1,000 for such an indefinite piece of land." While the Court said the Maxwell Land Grant Company couldn't sue for land it couldn't prove it owned, the Court also had trouble with the fact that Dawson claimed he had made a deal for the land with three friends *two* years before the deed was actually drawn. All of this caused the Court to reverse the lower body and to remand the case back for a district court trial. Once again Dawson prevailed, and then, on appeal in the Territorial Supreme Court, the case finally was dismissed.

Dawson's ability to endure—four years' worth of legal headaches, in this instance—paid off with a great victory. "He won," affirms his granddaughter Delphine Dawson Wilson, "because he was honest." Despite the long-awaited success, Dawson continued to ranch his land and grow his apples. But in 1896 he sold half of the mineral rights on the property to his neighbors, Charles and Mary Chase Springer.

Meanwhile, at the other end of the Territory, another canny businessman, one C. B. Eddy, had been following with interest the legal battles up north and the coal fields that had provoked them.

Though Charles Bishop Eddy may have admired the steadfastness of J. B. Dawson, the two men had little in common. Born in New York in 1857, Eddy was an easterner who wore tailored suits and had no interest in ranching. He had landed in Colorado in the early 1880s and soon decided his calling in life would be promoting railroads. Someone once said of him: "Charles B. Eddy could dream up something, begin talking about it, would begin to believe in it himself, was then irresistible and could convince any skeptic." Eddy's dream had been to develop a railroad line from El Paso to White Oaks, New Mexico, where there reportedly was a good supply of coal. Eddy's El Paso & Northeastern Railroad began in

1897, but the White Oaks-Capitan vein turned out to be a dud. Undaunted, Eddy decided to hook up his railroad with the coal fields in Dawson, where he learned the seams were a good eight to eleven feet thick. First, he persuaded the Rock Island Railroad to extend a line from Kansas to a point west of Santa Rosa, New Mexico, where it would connect with his El Paso & Northeastern running up from Carrizozo. That done, Eddy then built a 132-mile spur from Tucumcari to Dawson, through the towns of Mosquero and Roy, and crossing the Atchison, Topeka & Santa Fe Railway at French, New Mexico, and the St. Louis & Rocky Mountain Railroad at Colfax.

Next on Eddy's agenda was to buy the Dawson coal fields, which he and a partnership named the Dawson Fuel Company did in 1901. From J. B. Dawson and the Springers, the new company purchased the mineral rights for $400,000 and, from Dawson, the town site for $5,000. Dawson insisted a burgeoning town be named in his honor, and Eddy and company had no objection. The total land came to about 23,000 acres, with an additional 15,000 to be added later. Dawson worked out an agreement to keep a small piece for himself.

Dawson—the town—had one small mine by now, which J. B. had formally opened in 1899 and which would become Mine Number One. More than 100 coke ovens were quickly installed, and their output went chiefly to fuel steel mills in Colorado and Pennsylvania. By late 1901, the town of Dawson had 200 people, 50 of whom worked at either Mine Number One or the newer Mine Number Two. Most of the coal went to the new town of Santa Rosa. A postmaster named George T. Pearl set up shop, taking over for J. B. Dawson's wife, Lavinia, who had handled the job out of the family ranch. A doctor, H. K. Pangborn, established a practice. The *Las Vegas Optic* for June 17, 1901, said, "It may be predicted that the

Looking up Main Street, ca. 1916

new town in Colfax County through his (Eddy) efforts backed by the railroad he represents, will become one of the most important towns in New Mexico.''

Forty children had enrolled in a school there in 1902, and the population climbed to 600. The following year, when the Polly, a two-coach train, started running three times a week from little French to Tucumcari, the town's status soared even higher. By 1904, mine and coke production had doubled.

As Eddy knew it would, Dawson's coke—pulverized coal heated in an airtight oven—soon caught the eye of the Phelps Dodge Corporation. Established in 1834 to supply New York City tin peddlers, P.D. had grown into a mammoth copper concern with extensive holdings in southeastern Arizona that included mines or smelters at Bisbee, Morenci, and Douglas. The timber that P.D. had been using in its Copper Queen smelter in Bisbee had all but run out, and a cleaner fuel, such as coke, was sought. A trip to Dawson revealed not only some of the best coking coal in the whole Raton bed, but a seam big enough to supply coal for the next 100 years. Dawson seemed such an attractive addition that P.D. took the first step in acquiring the town's coal by constructing the El Paso & Southwestern Railroad from Bisbee to El Paso. Early in 1905, Eddy, who knew an eager buyer when he saw one, offered for sale to Phelps Dodge the coal mines, plus the Dawson Railway, that 132-mile spur, and the El Paso & Northeastern, which by now had gone bankrupt. Its locomotives fueled by Dawson coal, P.D. could thus carry its own coke from one end of New Mexico to the other, and on into Arizona.

Discussions went on for months until suddenly Phelps Dodge decided to pull out of the deal. Company officials announced it would be better to run a rail line from Gallup, New Mexico, to the San Juan coalfields in northwestern New Mexico. Eddy, clever as a box of monkeys, jumped in. "Gentlemen," he told P.D., "your proposal sounds all right with one exception. San Juan coal won't coke." Unbeknownst to Phelps Dodge, Eddy had already analyzed the San Juan fields.

Finally, in July 1905, Phelps Dodge directors accepted Eddy's offer and paid $16 million. The deal made the company the second largest industrial railway owner in the United States. It also made P.D. owner of an entire community, one of approximately 200 company towns in the West. Phelps Dodge had no problem keeping the name of the place, but later changed the name of the coal operation to the Stag Cañon Fuel Company, after a landmark on the property. And Eddy's railroad, spur and all, became the El Paso & Southwestern. With a prominent company behind it now, Dawson by the end of 1905 had a population of 2,000, cottages everywhere, a new tipple where the coal was dumped, a washery where it was cleaned, and a power plant. In addition, 446 more advanced coking ovens were built to supplement the original 124. Two boiler houses were erected to supply steam, and a thirty-two-bed hospital went up. Railroad crews labored night and day to handle the flow of coal and coke to the main line. By 1906, thanks to its link with the railroad and its almost nonstop production, Dawson's population had swelled to 3,500. A dry goods store opened, the Southwestern Mercantile, run by a kindly, stout gent named T. C. Hill. Folks called him "Tennessee," but were always corrected. "It's Tennie C.," said Hill, who became a fixture behind the counter and was still working there twenty years later, long after the enterprise had become the company store. "The camp is busy as a beehive, thriving everyday. As the people crowd the new place an opening is made for them," said the *Trinidad Chronicle News* in 1906.

The town certainly made an opening for T. L. Kinney. Born in Indiana, Thaddeus Lincoln Kinney had grown up in southern Colorado, near Trinidad. Self-educated, he started out working in the offices of the Colorado Fuel and Iron Company in Walsenburg and moved from there to Madrid, New Mexico, a company town owned by the Albuquerque & Cerrillos Coal Company. Kinney was chief pay clerk in Madrid when Phelps Dodge, always on the lookout for loyal company men, brought him to Dawson in 1903. With his hooked nose, bald pate, and noble mien, Kinney soon became a familiar figure in town.

In 1908, the company made Kinney town supervisor and justice of the peace. Answering only to the general manager, Kinney would hold both positions for sixteen years. He served a similar tenure as secretary of Dawson's school board. However, Kinney's real task in those years of Dawson's growth was to keep order, which the new magistrate proceeded to do in his own inimitable fashion. In search of the proper amount to fine an offender, allegedly Judge Kinney would open a Montgomery Ward catalog, close his eyes, and point to an item on the page. The amount beneath Kinney's finger— say, $34 for a parlor organ—was the amount the guilty party owed for, say, stealing a ham.

Early days of the Dawson Hospital.

While most coal mining towns were among the worst of company towns, with poor labor-management relations, unsanitary conditions, and despicable housing, Dawson, with a seemingly content work force, clean water, and houses fronted by neatly cropped lawns and painted window boxes filled with flowers, appeared to be an exception, thanks in large part to Phelps Dodge's social conscience. P.D. had experience raising the standard of living in Bisbee and Morenci, Arizona, and the company had plans to do the same in Dawson. And yet there existed in Dawson throughout its formative years a rough-and-tumble flavor characteristic of any raw community experiencing the breakneck growth that accompanied the development of the West. Miners would arrive penniless and then suddenly have folding money to spend. In fact, during a four-year span, the community truly resembled a Wild West town.

The first recorded murder took place August 11, 1907, when a miner named John Jenkins was jailed after shooting the woman who had killed his brother, Tom. It seems that Tom Jenkins had gone to visit Lizzie Zeller, employed at Grace Ford's bawdy house in Coontown. Perched high up in Rail Canyon, Coontown then was Dawson's "sporting district." While drinking beer there, Tom and Lizzie got to wrestling over a revolver. The gun went off, and Tom was shot. When a distraught John Jenkins arrived on horseback, he fired three times at Lizzie. One bullet, authorities said, went through her, "temple to temple."

A sensational trial opened two years later in Raton, and three women "of Dawson resorts" were called as witnesses. Of the charge against him, John Jenkins said, "I think anyone would have done so under the circumstances." Jenkins eventually was acquitted. Lizzie Zeller, the *Raton Range* explained

in a footnote, had grown up in Las Vegas and had been on her own, earning a living since she was a young girl. "Her story is the old old story, of drifting aimlessly till she landed finally in the Grace Ford house at Dawson. And there came the end."

The end for three more Dawson residents came on March 19, 1909, in what the *Raton Range* called "one of the bloodiest tragedies in the history of this county." During an argument over some land located back in Italy, Antonio DiJulio shot his cousin Bartello in the abdomen with a rifle. Staggering down the street, Bartello sought refuge in the house of another cousin, Frank DiJulio. Antonio followed, and inside the house fired a second shot at Bartello, who was lying on a couch. That bullet hit Frank's wife, who was attending Bartello, and killed her instantly. This caused Frank to grab a dagger and fatally stab his brother on the doorstep. The DiJulio men were coke-pullers, the newspaper said, and added that "the family had always borne a good reputation."

"ANOTHER MURDER IN DAWSON" screamed a headline in the April 14, 1909, *Raton Range*. It seems that a boardinghouse owner named Jim Lenzini threw five men out of his place for not squaring their accounts. The ejectees returned, and according to the newspaper, "a scrap ensued." The "scrap" left Philip Marla with a bullet hole in his chest and Joseph Bella with one in his face.

That was the week for homicides in Dawson. On April 18, 1909, Thomas O'Neill shot and killed tipple boss Walter Byers during an argument. "O'Neill was hurried out of Dawson with a four-horse team," said the *Raton Range*, "accompanied by Deputy Sheriff Frank Vance, and brought to the Colfax County jail where he was incarcerated and charged."

Later that same year, the *Santa Fe New Mexican* told of

Dawson's first kidnapping. "An employee of the Phelps Dodge Mining Company, after stealing a horse, went to the home of pretty Marie Baca, snatched her from her bed, cut her hair with a big, dark knife and threatened to kill her if she did not go with him," wrote a reporter on September 1, 1909. Mrs. Baca's husband had been out of town when the abduction occurred. Her thirteen-year-old daughter was at home, however, and the girl, dressed in nightclothes, followed her mother and the kidnapper on foot, and then ran back to town and told the deputy sheriff. Arrested about twelve miles west of Dawson, Hercelluno Chávez was jailed in Raton. Said the *Santa Fe New Mexican*: "The people of the camp are up in arms over the affair and had the man been taken to Dawson, it would no doubt have caused mob violence."

Big-time crime continued in Dawson. On November 19, 1910, robbers knocked off the town's post office. They blew up the safe with nitroglycerin and, upon leaving, burned down the building. James Grimes and Dennis Hart, both from out of town, were subsequently charged with the robbery and a string of others across the Territory.

Even the area around Dawson wasn't spared. On May 14, 1908, three masked men on horseback held up the French train depot and rode off with $35,500—a payroll headed for Dawson's mine office. Neither the robbers nor the money was ever found.

With such unpleasant events happening and with the town getting regular visits from Phelps Dodge's top brass, something had to be done. Certainly violence and vice had never been condoned by the copper company. P.D.'s three founders —Anson Phelps, William Dodge, and Daniel James—were Calvinistic New Englanders who saw God's presence in every part of life, and would not tolerate the slightest bit of im-

morality. That philosophy had filtered down to Phelps Dodge higher-ups and finally to town supervisor T. L. Kinney. His mandate: clean up the town. Kinney hired a police chief, who had been a New Mexico mounted policeman, and six deputies. As a result crime, save for an occasional drunken brawl, disappeared almost immediately.

Something also had to be done about gambling. Baseball had become a major interest among Dawsonites, as people in the town had now begun to call themselves, and the wholesome involvement with the national pastime pleased Phelps Dodge—particularly when the local team won. But P.D. did not approve of the fact that gambling had become a chief part of the game. For example, when Dawson played Raton in baseball on June 16, 1907, the *Raton Range's* front-page account said: "The Dawson bunch were so confident that they came here with considerable money to put up on their favorites." The story revealed that Raton's victory caused Dawsonites to drop $500. A crackdown on betting was instigated, and gambling, like mayhem, soon declined.

With law-breaking under control, Kinney could tend to other affairs, which included managing the telephone exchange, electric lights, and house rentals. Indeed, helping early-day miners get settled required perhaps his biggest effort. Dawson thrived during its first years because Phelps Dodge could get inexpensive labor, and trainloads of workers arrived regularly from Nacozari, Mexico, where P.D. had an extensive mining operation. But, since the company reportedly wanted a mix of nationalities in Dawson, laborers were recruited all across southern and western Europe—by word of mouth or through the encouragement of a relative. Many of these immigrants were illiterate and frequently had their passage booked by business agents in Raton. *And what a*

Loreta, Dawson's first suburb, was located one mile northwest of town.

passage it often was! When Luigi Cincoronella left his home in Naples, a ship took him to New York and through Ellis Island, and then a train finally brought him to New Mexico, eighteen days later. Filled with hope of the American Dream and yet scared to his toes, he was led to the reassuring presence of T. L. Kinney. Some of those miners, like Cincoronella, settled on Capitan, a big hill near the center of Dawson named after the location in southern New Mexico where C. B. Eddy had originally looked for coal. Bolstered by this influx of labor, by 1916 Dawson was producing one-third of the state's coal.

As Dawson grew, Kinney helped its higher-salaried employees, such as James B. Morrow, who arrived in 1908 to serve as superintendent of the coke department, find homes in the downtown area, beginning a social insularity—downtown versus upcanyon—that would last for years. "You didn't see or hear of the mines or the people in them," says Isabel Kinney, who moved to Dawson in 1905 when she was thirteen. "All the Italians, they lived way up in the canyon." Isabel's father, Robert Hern, worked as a blacksmith, and though he held a blue-collar job, his daughter became part of Dawson's well-to-do when she wed T. L. Kinney in 1917. "I didn't know much about the Italians until Judge Kinney and I got married. When they got drunk or in fights, that was all I heard about."

Dawson continued to grow. When haircutter Sol Schwed arrived from Trinidad in 1906 to open the town's second barbershop, the event made page-one news. The stage line between Maxwell and Dawson became so crowded that people complained, as they did about the Reo Automobile line, a passenger service from Raton. When the stunning Opera House opened in 1907, New Mexico Governor George Curry showed up to make this speech: "More than twenty-three years ago I visited the site of Dawson. It was then one of the famous cattle ranches of the Southwest . . . today I find it the most prosperous coal mining town in all this great Southwest."

The Opera House, the town's spiffy venue for traveling stage shows, turned into such a centerpiece for community activity that Kinney moved his office into the building. In time, Kinney took on another job, that of booking stage acts—opera companies and vaudeville troupes—and, when moving pictures came along, Kinney brought those to town as well, earning a reputation among movie distributors as an arbiter of unquestionable taste.

For theater companies to consider Dawson on their schedules was unusual, for "coal camp" was not a term that normally connoted a great deal of sophistication. Thus, Dawsonites did not like the term. "We live in a town," they protested to a reporter in 1912, and indeed the "camp" had almost 4,000 people. "There was a smell of coal smoke in the air," remembers Alberta McClary, who first saw Dawson in 1908, "but we thought that's what all places were like." Boardinghouses replaced pioneers' tents, and bawdy houses shut their doors. Two saloons remained open, except on Sundays, and even then, according to Kinney, their rear entrances stayed closed. A sure sign of the town's progress came in the formation of neighborhoods. Dawson had seven mesas, each about 150 to 200 feet above the valley floor, and on each of the hills different nationalities settled, for reasons of social customs and language. Kinney understood this, just as he recognized that

some of the early mines had to be segregated—Greeks in one, Italians in another—since people worked easier with those they understood. But, in the neighborhoods or the mines, Kinney saw that absolutely no animosities existed. He labored to preserve this harmony, and it became one of Dawson's greatest attributes.

As Dawson grew, a livery stable opened and then a hotel. The latter, equipped with steam-heated rooms for fifty cents a night, mostly served traveling salesmen. A dentist hung out a shingle, and soon a tailor leased space, the only way a private enterprise could do business. "Dawson is the largest coal mining camp in the Territory," said the state mine inspector in 1910. His report put the total value of coal and coke shipped at more than $1.5 million, and he noted that workers in the mines included Japanese, Finns, French, and Swedes. About 75 percent of the non-English-speaking men could write. Three schools were in operation by 1910, and streets were lighted and curbed. Every need was met, it seemed. A bank handled foreign and domestic exchange, and town officials conscripted a musician named Maldo Coridori from Italy just to conduct a fledgling marching band of coal miners. For those residents with special cleaning needs, Hom Lee, called "Chinaboy" by just about everyone, started a laundry.

Business increased steadily in Dawson through 1916, when four new mines opened and production reached almost 1.5 million tons. In 1917, the Stag Cañon Fuel Company changed its name to the Phelps Dodge Stag Cañon Branch, and by the end of that year ten mines were running and the population of the town edged close to 5,000. The place had surely come a long way since J. B. Dawson planted his first apple tree there almost fifty years before.

And what of old J. B.? While he had loved his piece of

earth by the Vermejo, Dawson knew he couldn't live there forever, especially with those trains chugging in. Still, he arranged to hold out of the sale what he called his "home-place," 1,260 acres and the ranch, though he eventually deeded it all to the new owners in 1906. Dawson's wife, Lavinia, kept a grip on the old homestead herself for a while. In the contract with Dawson Fuel, she demanded exclusive rights for a ten-year period to sell milk in the new mining town. The purchasers agreed.

But a comfortable house and dairy cows were not enough to satisfy J. B. Dawson; he had to leave. "Grandpa couldn't live near a coal town with people traipsing all over his ranch," says his granddaughter. Coal miners, like barbed wire, had their good points, Dawson reckoned, but he didn't really want to be around them. In 1901, he turned the ranch operation over to a daughter and son-in-law and moved with Lavinia, three sons and their wives, a daughter and her husband, and a dozen grandchildren to Routt County in northwestern Colorado, where he had camped and fallen in love with the land, just as he had in New Mexico.

Though his belly was big now, his beard long and white, Dawson still was strong and adventurous and still wanted his family around him on his newest adventure. Once again he established a ranch, this one 2,400 acres in size and ninety miles from the nearest train whistle. The Colorado house had seven bedrooms, and in an upstairs front one granddaughter Delphine Dawson was born in 1903. "Grandpa was clannish and loved his family," she remembers, "but I don't think I ever sat on his lap."

Though he drew comfort from his new life, Dawson apparently continued to search. He conducted peculiar livestock experiments, trying in one to cross buffalo with Angus cattle. In 1910, he was baptized in a nearby river, an event that brought his old friend and partner Charlie Goodnight up to Colorado.

Now and then J. B. had word of Dawson the town, but he never went back to see how it had grown. "He wasn't sentimental," says his granddaughter. "Grandpa knew the place in New Mexico wasn't a cattle ranch any more, but he didn't seem to mind." "They're good people down there," he told his family of the ever-expanding city named in his honor.

Incredibly, Dawson's Colorado land turned out to also sit atop a coal field, a fact that Dawson once again did not know at the time of purchase. And once more he decided to sell to a buyer who wanted the mineral rights: the Victor-American Fuel Company. And, of course, Dawson, the able businessman, made a tidy profit, enough to retire to southern California, where, on December 27, 1918, he died at age eighty-eight.

Before J. B. Dawson left New Mexico, he built a small granite monument on a rise west of the Vermejo. Standing beneath a piñon tree, facing the valley he loved, the marker designated the graves of several family members, including some of the nine children J. B. had fathered. Before he died, Dawson let it be known that he didn't want to go back to that valley, much as he cared for it. "He knew it belonged to someone else," his granddaughter says. Never one for sentiment, John Barkley Dawson was buried in Los Angeles.

At the Phelps Dodge Mercantile, you could buy anything from hammers to fur coats.

Chapter Two

SOCIALIZING

*"You could walk down any street
and you could know just about
anybody."*

—Fred Bergamo

It's a fine, bluebell of an afternoon in Dawson, just a cloud or two above Saltpeter Peak, so all in all a good day to take a walk down Main Street. Dawson's few streets have names—Church, Vermejo, and Railroad being three—but Main, with a mouth that opens at the door of the town, with sidewalks and shade trees and a string of significant businesses, is the inspiriting force of the community.

Heading north from the entrance of Dawson, our first stop is that three-story, red brick building, the stately monolith with the overhang and cornices, the pillars and posts, the ornate tilework and impressive etching across the front. It's not Saks Fifth Avenue, though some people think of it that way, and, well, just last weekend folks came all the way from Denver to shop at the Phelps Dodge Mercantile, or the Mercantile, or, as most everybody calls it, the store.

When it was built in 1913, the Mercantile became the biggest department store in New Mexico, and it's kept that title for some time now. Horace Beall, the manager, is that serious-looking fellow standing up there on the mezzanine, watching shoppers buy everything from hammers to fur coats. "We can supply your needs from beans to beef to bread," the store's slogan goes. "From mousetraps to tractors."

Although Dawson had a store as far back as 1902, an enterprise that eventually was transformed into the town's gymnasium, it was nothing compared to the Mercantile. When P.D. took over in 1906, the company did not like Dawsonites to shop elsewhere, and stories exist of officials guarding the portal to town and confiscating from residents any out-of-town purchases. Shopping from a mail-order catalog was not encouraged, either. By 1930, however, restrictions had been relaxed. It's true that the Mercantile seldom offered bargains, forcing Dawsonites on occasion to drive to Raton or elsewhere to save money. But the company store didn't gouge, either.

You've got to appreciate the sumptuousness of this place. Aren't the big display windows stunning? They should be, for P.D. brings in decorators from Kansas City to sharpen things up. There are regular fashion shows here, and they say the ladies' ready-to-wear is among the best in the West.

Let's start by going down in the basement for a moment. That ice plant down here can churn out an astonishing 5,000 pounds every twenty-four hours. Ice is a mainstay of a Dawsonite's home, for perishables are bought daily, and only late in the town's life will electrical refrigeration make an appearance.

On the main floor is clothing ($35 for a fine suit) and groceries ($8 for 100 pounds of sugar) and a butcher shop ($.20 for a pound of beef). There's also a hardware department and a pharmacy. That marble staircase leads to the mezzanine, where there's furniture for sale, a bakery, and where the offices are located. Out back sits a fleet of delivery trucks—by 1919, sixty people will work for the store and its three branches in Dawson. A railroad siding runs up to the dock there, and that small outer building in this cradle-to-grave operation happens to be the town morgue.

There's nothing on the roof of the store except the word "DAWSON" in twelve-foot-high letters, painted there for airplanes to see, a few of which actually landed in a field south of town in the early 1920s.

Say what you want about a company store owning someone's soul, but when there are strikes in the coal mines, Dawson's Mercantile is vital, for miners would go hungry if the store didn't advance credit, usually through scrip, a familiar book of little coupons. But nobody really goes hungry in Dawson: it isn't unusual, say, for a mother of thirteen children to come into the Mercantile twice a month and buy 150 pounds of flour, 100 pounds of potatoes, and 25 pounds of lard.

The store is a place to keep up with town affairs by visiting across the counter, and with world affairs by reading the latest copy of *Liberty*. The store also is a spot to simply meet new people. Dawson schoolteacher Emogene Chase, out on a shopping trip one day, met a jut-jawed ex-football player-turned-miner named Juan Herrera in the store. Herrera asked her for a date—they went to the Opera House—and fifty years later they're still married.

Across Main Street huddles the Snake, the best-known saloon in town. There are other bars, such as Trani's, which sports a pool table, and Primaveri's, which everybody calls Bocho's because you can find a game of boccie outside. But those places are up the road a piece, toward the mines. Holding court this day on a Snake bar stool is, as usual, Terence Scanlon, an electrician who keeps the fans going at the mines. Scanlon, if you haven't noticed by now, has a map of Ireland for a face and is the father of ten children. He's a storyteller who knows Spanish, and at any moment now he'll stand up and recite Omar Khayyám's *The Rubaiyat*. Every bar should have a Terence Scanlon.

Peek into the Snake's back room and you'll find a cozy card chamber with a potbellied coal stove, sawdust on the floor,

Everybody's favorite saloon, the Snake.

and town bigshots in attendance. That boisterous Scotsman over there is Andrew Keddie, a manager at the Mercantile. How do we know he's Scottish? Listen: "By dom, ye better drink up."

Even during Prohibition the Snake saw a brisk business. Bootlegging and moonshining occurred in Dawson, as evidenced by the large quantities of sugar and hops sold at the company store at the time. All the bars in town do well, in fact, for rare is the miner who doesn't drink on his way home from work. Indeed, Phelps Dodge is not particularly concerned about the drinking habits of its employees. The company is far more interested in maintaining a happy work force.

We're back on Main Street again, moving past the Staff House, where P.D. officials, visiting from New York or Arizona, stay during inspection tours. Then we pass the Bank of Dawson, not run by Phelps Dodge but as a branch of the First National Bank of El Paso, chartered by the state in 1914. Inside, you'll find diligent cashier Don Secrest, counting coins as usual. The bank closed in 1931, and, before it liquidated its assets, managed to pay off most depositors. If they couldn't use scrip, miners paid in cash, so they had little use for a checking account anyway. Through the years, the Bank of Dawson weathered all sorts of financial storms, as well as the 1923 mine explosion. A few days after that tragic event, the bank ran this ill-timed ad in the town newspaper: "Without warning, something may happen that will stop your income." The bank later reopened as the post office, and surely no other building in New Mexico handles more mail from Italy and Yugoslavia.

That big structure across from the bank and up the street a few doors is the hospital, and the building next to it is the dispensary, both designed by Henry C. Trost, a prolific Southwest architect whose stately and durable style characterizes several Dawson landmarks. Say hello to Crozier Hart, the head physician of a medical complex that boasts twenty-six beds, two surgical centers, modern X-ray equipment, complete labor and delivery rooms, a pharmacy, and a dental office.

There have been several doctors in Dawson, including Frank Diver, a wonderful professional who practiced for twenty years in the town in the days before penicillin and sulfa drugs. Diver would sit at the bedside of a patient for long periods of time. Payment? Every month a P.D. employee would pay the company a small fee—a dollar or two—and this entitled him to full medical benefits. The son of a Raton physician, Hart has been in Dawson a long time, too. A hefty gent, trained in orthopedics, Hart acts gruff, and that voice, *"Whaddya want?"* could scare the hide off a bison. But he is a good person when you get to know him—why, his wife, Ruth, has taught piano in Dawson forever. Hart loves to attend Hispanic weddings, particularly the parties in private homes afterward, affairs that he invites himself to in order to gorge on *carne adobada*. (In truth, wedding invitations in Dawson aren't necessary anyway.) And, as far as a bedside manner goes, Hart's really quite giving when it counts: when a rock from a cave-in crushed Dave Lucero's leg, gangrene set in, and everybody in town figured Dave was a goner, Doc Hart calmly stepped in and saved the young miner's life. So grateful was Dave that he wound up working as an orderly in the dispensary.

Next door, on the second floor of the dispensary, C. W. Hoover has been practicing dentistry for as long as anyone can remember. Chester Hoover's a cat lover, and he'll pull a tabby's teeth in a shake. Loves to chew tobacco, too, and you'll notice he spits juice in a corner as he trudges up the dispen-

On payday the Main Office was a busy place.

sary's stairs. Hoover and his young protégé, Bill Saul, who grew up in Dawson, don't work for P.D., as Hart does. Still, the dentists don't charge much—$2 for an extraction, $4 for a filling, maybe $30 or so for dentures.

There are nurses about the medical center. As early as the 1920s, in fact, Phelps Dodge employed in Dawson a public health nurse who made home visits to check on vaccinations and sanitary conditions—''To ensure healthier, happier homes,'' explained P.D. Comprehensive prenatal care also was offered in Dawson, long before it was provided in other places.

Back across Main Street again we come to the Main Office, Phelps Dodge's branch headquarters in Dawson, known as the Stag Cañon Fuel Company. The general manager works here—he's usually someone P.D. rotates over from Arizona. There are desks, too, for the auditors and the sales agents, the men who sell Dawson's coal (and coke when it was produced) to the outside world. That busy, wavy-haired fellow in the front there is Celso Chávez, the chief mine clerk. He's in charge of payroll. Celso grew up in Dawson, and he knows everybody. If you want to get paid, you line up outside the Main Office every other Friday and look for Celso. Payday's a crazy time. On a big table in the office, Celso and Mac McClary, the chief clerk in bookkeeping, and some others, stack money. Bills are piled almost to the ceiling. In time, the people in the Main Office put each man's earnings in an envelope, along with a receipt that shows how much cash he's due, minus things like rent, electricity, and medical.

At the rear of the Main Office is the telephone office, and the small woman working the switchboard there is Goldie Whiteley. By 1915, long-distance calls had been made from the depths of Dawson's mines to Raton and Santa Fe, and there already were a handful of company phones up top. Residential telephones started to appear in the early 1920s. But the telephone system in Dawson never has been terribly sophisticated. The first Dawson directory, published in 1942, ran only eight pages. And the phones themselves never have had dials. What you do is ring up the switchboard, and Goldie will ask what number you want and you'll tell her, say, Domenic Salvo, at 822, and Goldie will plug you in.

We're at the Sweet Shop now, and there's young Bob McClary, mixing carbonated water and syrup behind the counter. Bob's managing the place while he goes to high school. Shakes, malts, sundaes and double scoops—that's what people buy here, along with tobacco and candy. Ice cream's king, though. Every other Friday—payday—the Sweet Shop sells as much as 120 gallons of ice cream. And everybody flocks here after a basketball game in the gym or before a movie up at the Opera House. In fact, you could go into the Sweet Shop even on a Sunday morning and see two miners hunched over one of the little round tables, licking chocolate ice cream cones.

The Sweet Shop is the only hangout for Dawson kids. Come in here after school and you can hear ''String of Pearls'' on the jukebox, you can play one of the punchboard games for a nickel and try to win a pecan roll, or you can eat a banana split for thirty cents.

Next stop is the Opera House, which, like the Mercantile, has a distinctive architecture that features cornices and keystones, a cupola facing and a fancy lintel, and cost $40,000 to build. The building's nearly as much a hub of activity as the store. You know what's going on inside the Opera House this night by the movie billboard out front—William Powell and Myrna Loy, starring in *Crazy Love*. Climbing the impos-

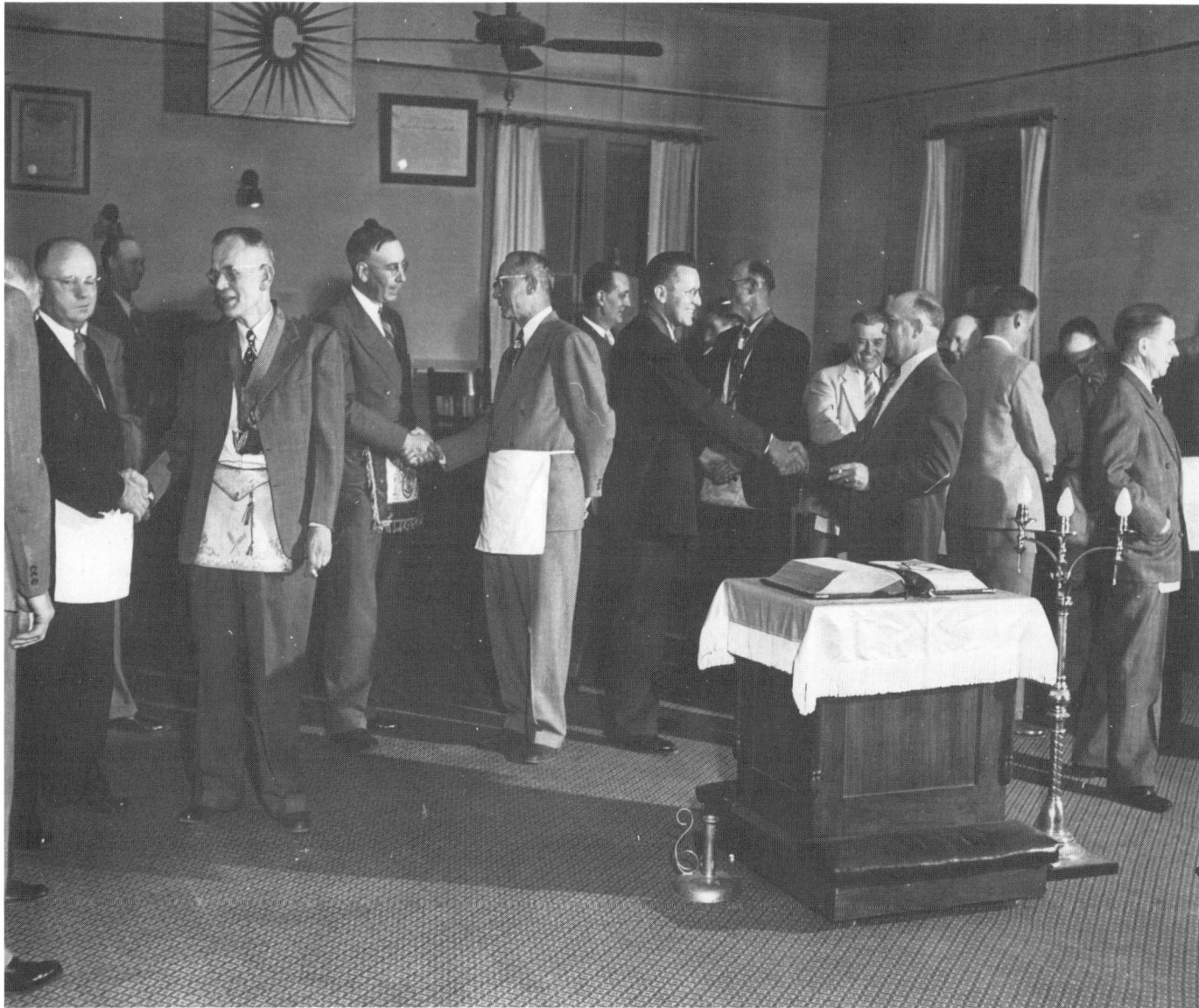

The Masons were one of many fraternal organizations that met in the Opera House.

ing steps and entering, you begin to smell something. That's P. K. Carson's cigar. Bow-tied town supervisor Paul Carson runs the Opera House, among other jobs, and you can usually tell where he is in town by that ever-present cigar between his teeth. Some people think Carson runs everything in Dawson. As director of the Welfare Department, he puts out the *Dawson News*, a weekly that will last from 1921 to 1929, the town's most bountiful years, when the population passed that of Raton, the county seat, a fact that was a source of much satisfaction. The *Dawson News* stresses cheerfulness in its articles, for Phelps Dodge, which owns the *DN*, wants nothing less than upbeat information for its employees. For example, whenever a young Dawson woman gets married, the *Dawson News* always says, "She is popular and has a wide circle of friends."

Carson also finds time to serve as scoutmaster, and he is in charge of housing, which places him in one of the town's most important roles, especially if you are a newcomer. Housing, however, isn't always available. When there are prosperous times in Dawson, there's usually a waiting list for homes, so some families double up. And when families get larger, as often happens in Dawson, bigger houses are sought and the waiting list is employed again. That list is ruled, some say with an iron fist, by Carson. Carson took over many of the duties performed by T. L. Kinney, who, some say, *lived* in the Opera House. Like a lot of men of the day, Kinney was devoted to his job. One afternoon in March 1924 he was found slumped over his desk at the Opera House, dead of an embolism at age fifty. The judge's funeral was held, naturally, in the Opera House.

The Opera House has about 350 molded, plywood seats, and legend has it that Enrico Caruso rendered *I Pagliacci*

here, but no proof exists. Oh, the place certainly had a name. In those early days when Dawson had a sizeable population, Chautauquas, minstrel shows, and vaudeville acts came through from the East Coast. Indeed, Dawson's was the only opera house between Kansas City and San Francisco, south of Denver at least, and Eddie Foy came here, as well as stage great May Robson. It was a gay place then, with a shoeshine parlor even, and Goldie Whiteley, now at the switchboard, used to play piano in the orchestra pit for such silent movies as *The Mark of Zorro*, starring Douglas Fairbanks, which opened on February 12, 1921, and cost twenty-two cents to see. When talkies came around, and Jeannette McDonald and Nelson Eddy seemed to turn up every week, Poodle Hancock changed reels up in the booth, and industrious Bob McClary swept piñon shells off the floor.

The Opera House is not simply a movie theater. All the school plays and operettas and band concerts are performed here. Graduation is held onstage, as is just about any big event, even unconventional ones: one year the junior class in high school, needing money for a prom, put on a style show in the Opera House, a fashion parade that rivaled anything the Mercantile could do. Only this performance featured boys wearing girls' clothes.

A room off the Opera House's front entrance serves as Dawson's polling place. For many years Dawson voted mainly Republican, influenced surely by the top officials in town. T. L. Kinney, for example, put in several terms as a GOP delegate to the state convention in Santa Fe. By the mid-1930s, however, the town, like much of New Mexico's large Hispanic population, had swung over to Roosevelt and his Democratic ideals. On the top floor of the Opera House, lodge groups—Eastern Star, the Knights of Pythias, Woodmen of the World, Rotary, Foresters, Moose, Italian Masons, Alianza Hispaña, the Croatian Society, you name it—hold meetings. Down in the basement you'll find two bowling alleys, and, wouldn't you know it, P. K. Carson is captain of one of the bowling teams.

But there is more to a town than stores and offices, of course. People live in Dawson. In tents at first, hundreds of them. And then in ethnic boardinghouses, particularly single miners and those waiting for their wives to come over from Europe. The boardinghouses are homey: go to the one run by Greeks on the feast day of St. Basil and you may never want to leave—and probably can't, for all the ouzo you've drunk. Others, like Lash's, Primaveri's, and Brozovich's, have bars and banquet rooms and elaborate kitchens where lunches are prepared, and maybe a shower room outside. Dawson also means homes. Never a collection of shacks set helter-skelter on various hillsides, as found in most coal mining towns, and never a *camp*, Dawson is organized. Oh, some families had to share a home in the beginning, but most residences in town are single-family dwellings, presided over, of course, by P. K. Carson.

If Dawson is anything, it is a town of neighborhoods. Though Dawson is known as the place where people get along, segregation typically exists in those neighborhoods. Simply, people in Dawson want to live among their own nationality. The Italians and Slavs and Greeks settled most of Number Seven Camp, established to serve Mines Seven, Eight, and Nine. Italians and Hispanics make up Capitan, both Old Capitan and New. More Hispanics dominate Five Hill. For the most part, Anglos are downtown, in the houses that edge Main Street, often referred to as "Back Street," and the homes along Church Row and behind that thoroughfare, seven square blocks in all. If you go way up past Mine Number Six, you'll probably meet the most pleasant black man, Charley Burrell. He'll be out hauling water with his half-dozen or so black neighbors, in a nice place with a terrible name: Coontown. Save for an abbreviated Ku Klux Klan incident, racial problems in Dawson are nonexistent, because Phelps Dodge will not tolerate discrimination.

Like the pages of a calendar, other neighborhoods in Dawson come and go, such as Loreta, a tidy suburb up the canyon that is spelled variously Loretta, Lorita, and even Loretto. Some unofficially named locales like "Tanktown," "Chihuahua," "Carucco," and the "V" also exist. Several houses even surround the Phelps Dodge Ranch, the Diamond D, across the river, ably managed for more than thirty years by John O'Brien. Built originally by J. B. Dawson, the central ranch house is an imposing antebellum-like structure, with almost a dozen bedrooms, a broad balcony, formal dining rooms, and maids to clean every inch. South of the ranch, a dairy, with fifty-two Holstein cows imported from Arizona, stays busy enough in peak years to produce 140 gallons of milk a day. The ranch's 1,400 acres of alfalfa are planted to feed the mine mules. There's also an 80-acre fruit orchard, a monstrous garden, thoroughbred hogs, plenty of good grazing land for cattle, plus the largest man-made irrigation system in New Mexico. Phelps Dodge bought the ranch and dairy not to make money but to feed the town.

When P.D. took over Dawson, the company tore down shanties near the entrance to town and tried to give a uniformity, an authenticity, to the community. Dawson houses, you'll notice, are set mostly in rows, and many are wood frame, particularly the older ones, though a number of the houses are coke breeze block, a type of porous cinder block manufactured in town. All the houses are simple but well-built units of one, two, or three bedrooms. What they have in common most is color: all are white with green trim. Heated by coal, naturally, every house has bins behind it for storing the bituminous ore, which is also used for cooking. Dawsonites like to tell the story about a traveling salesman who wandered into town in the 1940s and tried to interest residents in buying propane. He was last seen running for his life.

Rent is as little as $8.50 a month for a four-room house, plus another $3.00 or $4.00 for water, electricity, and fuel. Concerning the electricity: P. K. Carson watches the meters like a goshawk, and if someone's light usage is, say, a few clicks more than his neighbor's, Carson and his cloud of cigar smoke are on the way to find out why.

For half of Dawson's life, indoor plumbing did not exist in town. But about 1930 things started to change, and most of the new houses now have sinks, bathtubs, and toilets. Along about that same year some Maytag washers appeared in Dawson. But a number of families still use washtubs and scrub boards, moving supper pots to the back of the stove each evening and bathwater pots to the front, in order to make sure a husband has his bath when he comes home from the mines. Even late in Dawson's life, some miners' wives still were boiling their husbands' clothes in lye to get them clean as well as making their own soap by mixing lard and lye. Although most Dawson homes had radios, the town never did see the beaming face of a television screen.

You can fix up your house, and many residents, with Phelps Dodge's blessing, have done makeovers both inside and out. And when you want the exterior of your home painted— white with green trim, of course—P.D. has it done for you. Many Dawson houses have numerals on them, though they're not always in sequence. But, really, a Dawsonite doesn't need numbers to find anybody. He knows where just about everybody lives. Nobody says John Bizyak lives at 2201. You say he lives in the third house back on that hill over there.

Much of the social life in Dawson revolves around clubs. Clubs are everywhere, it seems, for Dawsonites are joiners and it's something Phelps Dodge encourages in the company's spirit-of-togetherness design. Over there, at Hazel Pool's house on Church Row right at this moment the Eightsome Bridge Club is meeting. And last week the Dawson Book Club gathered there because, well, Dawson doesn't have a public library, which may be the only thing it doesn't have. (You can check books out of the high school library, however.)

To get to some of those club meetings and other places in town, most Dawsonites walk. Though there are no exact city limits, the town is, after all, only about thirty square miles. You walk to school, you walk to work. But many Dawsonites drive, especially on weekends, and the *Dawson News* records *every* motor trip *every* citizen makes. Cars first chugged into town just before World War I, and kids used to beg the postmaster of that day, George Bradford, to give them rides in his big red Buick. By the 1920s, cars were everywhere in Dawson. Times were good, and most miners found they could buy a car on time, and they did. Many miners bought a new car every year, a fact that the *Dawson News* did not neglect. From the February 23, 1922, edition: "Mr. Frank Vidano of Loreta is the owner of a new Dodge car." By 1928, approximately 750 people in Dawson had cars. There were 4,500 people in the town that year, so that means every sixth person had wheels—Studebakers and Nashes, giant four-door sedans and touring cars. Albert Van Dyke's Dawson Garage and Filling Station, down on Main Street, specialized in Erskine cars. Of course, with so many new and inexperienced drivers, accidents occurred. Throughout the early days of cars in the town, Dawson children were regularly run over by mistake, and cars repeatedly sailed off various bridges. Although the *Dawson News* editorialized constantly about the need for automobile safety, cars continued to slam into each other, to strike pedestrians and trees and, on at least one occasion, even a horse-drawn wagon.

As in any small town, anonymity has always been nonexistent in Dawson. Everybody knows everybody else, and, because the town has a common thread that runs through it, there certainly are no outcasts. If a man hobbles down Main Street, nobody thinks anything about it, because lots of men hobble from mine accidents. When Arthur Lucero, a young victim of cerebral palsy, crawls down the street, people merely smile and wave.

And, as in any small town, everybody knows everybody else's business. Most of the scandals in town have to do with the relationships between men and women: the postmaster gets shot during a scuffle with his wife; the high school principal courts a student twenty years younger; a jealous wife poisons sandwiches she puts in her miner-husband's lunch bucket. In Dawson's raw days, a spouse would often leave town for one mysterious reason or another. A new job? A new life? Hard to say. Those were the days, too, of mail-order brides, and Dawson had its share. For instance, a miner would come to town, start working, and then send back to the old country for a woman. Maybe he knew her, maybe he didn't, but one thing he did know: he was lonesome. One Greek miner paid a well-known compatriot named Gus to send for Gus's niece. The girl arrived and stayed at Gus's boardinghouse, but, instead of spending time with the miner who had bought her passage, she fell in love with somebody else. When the miner demanded that Gus pay him back, Gus refused. The disappointed suitor eventually ambushed Gus and shot him dead. The custom of acquiring unknown brides —and the occasional violence that followed—stopped when Dawsonites became proficient in English and learned they could date and marry other nationalities.

But marrying outside of your nationality didn't come easily, even in Dawson's last years. Exiting church one day in the late 1930s, Josephine Marcelli met José Andazola, and they soon began dating. Josephine's father, however, preferred that she see an Italian rather than a Hispanic. The couple were in love, and so in 1941 they eloped to Raton and then came back to Dawson to live on Capitan with José's mother and family. "My father was so angry," says Josephine. "He sent word to me that I could visit my mother if he wasn't there. I really missed my father. We were real close; I had helped him in the garden and even chopping wood. I didn't want it to go on; Dawson was such a small place." Finally, after seven months, Josephine and her husband were invited to a New Year's Day party at her old home. "When we went in, it was all over. My father apologized. 'I have forgiven you,' he said. He told me he missed me, too. There was a lot of hugging and a lot of love. In later years he told me how much he cared about Joe."

Not everybody in Dawson saw it that way, unfortunately. Nellie Wilson, a tough Scottish woman, believed that if you weren't a Scot, you were a foreigner. Nellie ran her daughter's boyfriend out of Dawson with a shotgun. Nellie hadn't minded that her daughter was pregnant; she just didn't like it that the baby's father was Italian. Couples of different nationalities were sometimes forced to date on the sly. "Sneak around," it's called in Dawson. Gabe Trujillo would sneak around with Eva Mary Smock, a Scottish girl from downtown. Bob McClary would sneak around with a Greek girl from Number Seven Camp. Victor Padilla didn't want his daughter, Grayce, to sneak around with a Mexican boy because the Padillas, Victor announced proudly, are from Spain. So sometimes these young people who would sneak around would run off to get married. Often this caused a fuss for a while, as happened with Josephine and José Andazola, but much of the time it was an occasion for celebration, for Dawsonites realize the special bond they have. When Emogene Chase married Juan Herrera in 1942, in Dawson's St. John the Baptist Catholic Church, half the town turned out to share in their happiness. There are sad stories, however, and surely one of the most heartbreaking occurred when Margaret Mary Beall married Tony DiLorenzo in 1947 and Margaret Mary's mother, so incensed, refused to speak to her daughter, an only child, for almost forty years.

"We gossiped some," admits Anna Lucero, born and reared in the town, "but Dawson wasn't a sinful place. There wasn't any bed-hopping." Anna herself generated some over-the-back-fence talk when, in 1935, instead of graduating from high school, as she was scheduled to do, she got married because she was pregnant. "Me and Charlie Mataya had been going together for three or four years. Was that a big deal? Well, Dawson was predominantly Catholic, so I guess it was. But other girls got pregnant then, too. People said it must have been something in the water."

Then there is the matter of affluency. Money—or the lack of it—keeps people in different neighborhoods and in different financial situations. And yet nobody is very poor or very rich in Dawson. There never has been, for instance, any begging in the streets, not even during the Great Depression, for there is almost always some work available in the mines, even if only for a couple of days a week. Charity then, as well as crime, is almost unknown. Dawson is not faultless. In the earliest days, the few Chinese and Japanese in town were not allowed through the doors of the saloons. And it took a while for the mines to let a black man inside. Most of the school board members and most of the office staff are Anglo. But nobody notices, or at least nobody makes a big deal of it, for Dawson's fervent solidarity counts most. Shirley Bain lives downtown, and her father, Eddie, is a meat cutter at the Mercantile. She sometimes hears silly stuff about living "uptown," which is really downtown, because when you live uptown you have an indoor toilet. The Bains may live uptown, but they don't own a car and can't afford one. As a teenager, Shirley is bothered a bit by this; she'd just like to *sit* in a car. But the nice thing is that the Bains know they can get a ride from anyone in town anytime they want. Cooperation between neighbors is characteristic of Dawson.

Bob McClary lives with his family in a comfortable three-bedroom house downtown. Although Bob's father has a good job in the Main Office, Bob gets along with every kid in town, no matter where those kids live or what their parents do. One of Bob's best friends is Joe Rios. Joe's father is a section hand, and they live up at Old Capitan. The other day Bob noticed that Joe had on a pair of snappy, high-top shoes. More than anything in the world, Bob now wants a pair of "Joe Rios shoes."

For both those with money and those without it, no better manner of socializing takes place in Dawson than Field Day. Various nationalities in Dawson have always observed their own special holidays, such as Mexican Independence Day on

*Aerial view of Dawson
taken from the southwest.*

*A Field Day in Dawson
involved the whole community.*

September 16, or Cinco de Mayo, or Columbus Day. But the day that brings all of Dawson together is the day of the community picnic.

Dawson had gathered for town picnics before, usually on the Fourth of July, but the first Field Day was held September 29, 1923. Surely it was conceived by Phelps Dodge to take townspeople's minds off the horrific mine explosion earlier in the year. The mines would be closed this day, and the town's Welfare Committee, which was in reality the Stag Cañon Branch of Phelps Dodge Corporation, made no bones that the picnic was to develop a stronger community spirit. It was to be "a day of recreation, entertainment and good fellowship," declared the *Dawson News*.

Those early Field Days started with a parade of cars—decorated ones or new ones that residents simply wanted to show off—down Main Street. That would be followed by a football game, a baseball game, and a soccer match, with breaks for free sandwiches and coffee. Then there would be swimming races and all sorts of goofy events, such as girls' boxing, a fat man competition, rolling pin throwing, a needle-threading race, and a husband-calling contest. Two thousand people showed up for the 1926 Field Day. The following year, Elsie Mangino was elected Field Day Queen, after capturing 218,000 votes through an obviously stuffed ballot box, and won a $75 first prize. Elsie was an eighteen-year-old employee of the Sweet Shop, and, according to the *Dawson News*, "Her amiable disposition has won a legion of friends."

By 1928, Field Day, always held in late September, had gained such prominence that New Mexico Governor Richard C. Dillon pitched the first ball at the picnic's baseball game. And Dillon didn't merely stay a moment to shake a few hands; he remained in town until Louie Savio's community band had finished "Home, Sweet Home" at the end of a dance that ended an exhausting day.

Field Day is enjoyed by everyone, but surely the miners like it most. It's a chance for them to flex their muscles in view of the whole town. The nail-driving contest always brings oohs and aahs from the womenfolk. So does the coal-shoveling competition. In 1928, George Starkovich, from Mine Number Nine, shoveled a two-ton pile of coal in ten minutes and forty seconds. There are tugs-of-war between the mines' "inside" and "outside" men, but perhaps the most prestigious event of Field Day is the first-aid contest, for nothing in Dawson is considered as important as safety. Janet Wilson Hancock remarks: "One year I was on a team that practiced two to three times a week for the community picnic. There were four or five women's teams entered. We splinted broken bones, fixed necks, did artificial respiration, put people on stretchers. We were rated by judges, and our team won. We each got $10, which was about the most money I had ever seen."

When Field Day ends each year, Dawsonites gather up their baseball gloves, coal shovels, and tin cups, the latter brought along for free coffee refills, and head for home and another workday. Some drive to those homes, offering rides as they go. The rest walk, some beneath the cottonwoods, locusts, and elms along Main Street, others by way of shortcuts across the river or through the hills and past houses where no stranger ever lives.

Chapter Three

GROWING

*"You didn't need money to have
fun, like kids today think you do."*

—Henry Reza

"Hey, Mookie!"
"Moo-kie!"
"MOO-OOO-KEEEE!"
There was "Brains" and "Birdseed" and "Weasel" and
"Coomy" and "Snake" and, of course, "Mookie." Growing
up in Dawson so often meant acquiring a nickname. Some
of the handles were obvious, such as "Lefty" or "Red" or
"Skinny" or "Chubby." But others had a story of their own.
For instance, if your Dawson friends saw you holding a baby,
you might wind up being called "Doc," as Ernest Bergamo
did. And not just Doc for a few months; you were Doc for-
ever. If you were Ernest Mares, and your given name was Neto,

but an eight-year-old pal mispronounced it, you were "Nebs."
And what of Mookie? Poor little Henry Peppin. The kid clears
his throat one day, brings up a bit of mucus, and he's branded
for life.

Seventy-five years after he was born in Dawson, Bill Hancock still lives in northeast New Mexico. Every once in a while
Hancock goes to Raton to run errands, and one day there not
long ago, Hancock was studying the hammers in a hardware
store when all of a sudden he heard someone shout something from another aisle. "Hey! Poodle!" the voice called.
"POO-OOO-DULLLL!" Hancock smiled, looked up, and
wondered what Dawsonite was recollecting the 1920s, when

he was a kid and got a nickname that is perhaps one of the best-known in Dawson annals.

Hancock blames his brother Buster for the whole thing. Bill was born small, and just after birth Buster took one look at him and said, seemingly for all of Dawson to hear, "Why, he looks just like a poodle dog!"

People such as Poodle Hancock explain a lot about Dawson. Being given a nickname—"Chango" or "Puso" or "Growlo"—and having it stick reveals the extraordinary fondness that people in the town had and still have for one another. Dawson may be gone, but the nicknames are one strong way the place endures. The nicknames, even the ones that describe physical characteristics, have nothing to do with ridicule. Rather, the sobriquets should be interpreted as badges of membership, to be used only by those who lived in Dawson. The names then are signs of respect and to be understood in this fashion: listen, I spent my childhood in a carefree place where everyone liked me and where we had a great time and where we frequently called each other silly things. But listen, it was all done with genuine affection.

Maybe it was because Dawson was a company town, but if you were a kid there was always plenty to do in the community. Not necessarily organized things, for it is really the unorganized, the free things, that are remembered most. Every neighborhood in town, from Capitan to Five Hill, had a favored spot, a level and smooth patch of dirt, where kids would lay down a small piece of stretched-out rabbit skin, put their knuckles on that rug, and shoot marbles. When you weren't playing marbles, you might be having a rubber-gun fight. Rubber gun? You simply cut out a band from an inner tube and then attached that strip to a piece of wood, a piece shaped like a pistol, with a notch in the top of it. Then you stretched the band back to the notch and fired. If you hit a person, he was out of the game. Yes, most every competitor remembered to close his eyes.

There were games of hopscotch and capture-the-flag, and everybody in Dawson had a tire. If you went to visit somebody's house, you took your tire with you, rolling it alongside you as you walked. The brave children—and girls usually were the bravest—would climb inside a tire and have somebody send them down the hill from Capitan, spinning so hard and bumping so much they felt like their insides had been taken out, stirred about, and then stuffed back.

Tire-rolling, sad to say, is a lost pastime. So is storytelling. In the evenings, after dinner, Dawson families would gather on their front porches and tell stories. Whatever happened to storytelling? Whatever happened to front porches? Grandparents would sit there and, in halting English, tell about the old country. And their grandchildren would *listen*. Children in Dawson weren't afraid to play outside in the dark because adults were right there—on that porch. Oh, once in a while an elderly Hispanic woman in Dawson might get upset with her kids out after dark because *La Llorona*, the Weeping Woman of Mexican folklore who is lamenting the loss of her children who were drowned in a river, was said to be out and about, even though the crying sounded just like the wind coming down the canyon. In fact, when rumors spread that *La Llorona* might possibly be in town, the company store sold out of flashlights.

From the very earliest days of the town, growing up in Dawson was almost wondrous. For a newcomer entering Dawson seventy-five years ago, the town must have appeared absolutely entrancing, what with the coke ovens burning night and day, and the *clankety-clank* sound of coal cars feeding

Boy Scouts held a prominent place in Dawson.

those ovens, and the mule-drawn wagons pulling loads, and the kids playing in the dirt streets. Phelps Dodge did much to organize activities for kids, starting with the Scout House, which went up in 1923 atop Gobbler's Roost. Built of coke breeze blocks, inside was a kitchen, locker room, and stone fireplace, and the house was always busy. Indeed, during the 1920s Dawson had *two* Boy Scout troops. The Scouts had a basketball team, a band, a summer camp, and even held first-aid competitions. President Warren Harding was so impressed by the enthusiasm of the town's Scouts that he sent a letter saluting Dawson. Maybe the high point of those years for the Scouts came in June 1923, when a Dawson Boy Scout named David Hardin jumped into the Cimarron River and rescued a small girl being swept downstream.

As Scouts discovered, along with just about every other young person, the wide-open spaces around Dawson offered the greatest playground imaginable. Sitting in the middle of a giant canyon, Dawson was surrounded by visually stunning hills teeming with wildlife. The hunt was on: some kids had traplines, but many owned an old, single-shot .22, so beat up it took a penknife to remove the spent shells. There were plenty of jackrabbits to aim those .22's at, and adults, such as George Fenlon, the school superintendent, loved to lead expeditions. Some hunting parties went out unchaperoned, of course, such as when Bill Saul and Carlyle Vickers went hunting one afternoon, and, thinking a giant bird was going to swoop down and pick them up, opened fire on a golden eagle.

Growing up in the great Dawson outdoors meant scrambling up and down mesas, like Elephant Rock, and through canyons, like Van Bremmer. It meant making "cabins" in the ridges just outside of town—carved-out spots in the hillside, which a boy or girl would cover over and "furnish" with a cot or a stove and some boxes to make it look like home. It meant playing hopscotch (*Step on a crack, you'll break your mother's back*) in front of Central School or clambering *up* instead of sailing down the school's slide.

Was there anything better than a Dawson summer? July and August meant going to Cimarron Canyon to fish in the shade of the palisades, or over to the irrigation canals near Maxwell to get crawdads, filling up a gunnysack with them, and later at home boiling them in water and finally eating the lobster-like things. Summer meant going to the town swimming pool, or if you could not afford the dime it cost kids to get in, or even a pair of swimming trunks—and during the Great Depression, not that many people in Dawson could—it meant heading up to the Vermejo River, a couple of miles or so to where the river curved, and making a dam out of sand and rocks to construct your own swimming hole. Summer meant hiking out to the mile sign on the railroad tracks, where there stood a large grove of plums and choke-cherries to pick—or searching for gooseberries and *quelites*, or wild spinach. Summer meant going to the circus that would come to town bringing a Ferris wheel that would be set down in the baseball park, along with such sideshow oddities as "The Big Snake," a huge reptile that died during one performance in Dawson and whose owners blamed the town because the air was said to be too cold and the altitude too high.

Fall meant the arrival of the grapes, by truck or by train car, and that meant kids could help in the pressing and crushing of those grapes, which were used to make homemade wine. In many Dawson homes, especially during Prohibition, make-shift stills gave miners a chance to augment their wages. Fall meant Halloween, and that meant removing the furniture

School dances in a gymnasium were town-wide affairs.

For kids, summer afternoons meant the community swimming pool.

from Mr. Fenlon's front porch and putting it up on the church steeple and then waiting to hear him say, resignedly, the next day, "OK, you better get it down now." Halloween was also a time for tipping over outhouses, the standard-issue bathroom in Dawson for many years, and having the town marshal, the all-knowing L. O. Mace, nicknamed "Dick Tracy," or Mace's successor, Jack "The Shadow" Randall, take you to P. K. Carson, who was wiser than a treeful of owls. In Dawson, you didn't only get in trouble with the law, you got in trouble with the town, which was worse because most fathers worked for the company, which, of course, owned the town. "*State attenti!*" Italian mothers warned their children. "Be careful." It was said less out of worry about possible injury than concern for getting in trouble with the company, which

could cause a father to lose his job.

No youth in Dawson, however, did anything terribly malicious. Mace or Carson or anyone else in a town who took great pride in being neat and orderly would have been appalled to see something as awful as graffiti.

Winter's arrival—and the moderate snow that Dawson usually received—signaled closing off Church Row and using pieces of tin as sleds to slide down the little incline on that street. Or checking out the toboggans that Phelps Dodge owned, and trudging up Capitan with those boards. Winter, of course, also meant Christmas and that meant going to Tiptop, the hilly area between Loreta and Capitan, and cutting down your family's tree. Permit? Don't be absurd. For a Dawson child, Christmas meant going to the Opera House and walking onstage past the big Christmas tree to receive from a P.D. official a bag of candy and a small toy. For a brief period later, when that child was older, Christmas meant getting from P.D. a necktie or a pair of stockings. New Year's Eve meant a town dance at the gym, then midnight Mass at the Catholic church, then back to the gym for more dancing.

In spring, when rains came and the streets turned muddy, Dawson kids pulled out their homemade stilts and traversed the town. Spring meant catching rabbits and raising them as pets. Spring also meant creating kites out of newspaper and wooden box frames, gluing them together with flour and water, and then flying the craft in the alfalfa field that lay between the filling station and the Vermejo.

In any season, Dawson kids would, in the tradition of Andy Hardy, put on plays or shows in their garage, shed, or basement. All one needed was a sheet for a curtain and some stick matches for the price of admission. Having a good time might mean crossing the swinging bridge to Loreta or begging for a ride on the Polly, the El Paso & Southwestern Railroad's little passenger train that followed the coal cars' route to Tucumcari. A round-trip to Roy was a great way to kill a day; you could sit on the train's wooden seats and stare at the initials "EP&SW" on the door and imagine they stood for "Eat Plenty and Sleep Well." Fun for Dawson kids was simply where you found it. Jess "Chuy" Ponce and his buddy, Tony Arellano, used to go down to the cemetery and while away hours there at night. Jess would sit on his sister's grave, and Tony on his father's marker, and they'd spend the night talking. About what? About how brave they were. Henry Reza and his friends liked to go to the White Rocks, the sandstone outcropping on Capitan. There, at night, they would build a bonfire and roast marshmallows or potatoes,

look at the northern lights, sing, and tell ghost stories. When the food was gone and faces were charred, everybody went home, happy as ticks in a dog's ear.

Dawson girls did most of the things that the boys did, except receive nicknames, though Emma "Woozy" Wallace was an exception. Little Mary Calderone was the best marbles shooter in Capitan, maybe in all of the town. Dawson girls did things that boys weren't expected to do, too, such as help out when a baby brother or sister was being born in the home, which happened frequently in the camps that were far from the hospital or where the parents simply didn't trust doctors. For girls, too, there were dances in the gym after the basketball game. "Everybody went," says Lena Colaizzi Forte. "Adults and little kids, three, four years old. The young kids would dance on the side of the gym, and the others in the middle of the floor." Dawson girls also had parties, as this item from the *Dawson News* of the 1920s recounts: "Alice, the little daughter of Dr. and Mrs. W. Adams, celebrated her seventh birthday Tuesday by entertaining a company of her little friends in honor of the event."

Food and drink play prominent roles in almost every Dawson childhood memory. For Paul Brozovich, whose parents were Slavic, growing up meant watching his mother, Katarina, owner of a boardinghouse, cook up huge plates of kielbasa and sauerkraut, potica, and apple strudel. Fred Becchetti can still smell slices of warm bread and slabs of cheese on his kitchen table. Often there was homemade wine on those tables as well. Alice DiLorenzo used to watch her father, Domenic, brew what everyone called "Dago red" in the family cellar, and then keep small glasses filled with it at mealtime. Beer had its place in the home, too. Don Wilson's grandfather was a mule tender, and every payday he would give his wife a lit-

At one time Camp Fire provided Dawson girls with an outdoor experience.

tle manila envelope filled with cash and she would give him back a dime. Don would take that dime down to the Snake for his grandfather, get the old man's mining pail, the water pot he took with him underground, filled with beer, and bring it back home. "God help me," says Wilson, "if I spilled a drop."

Even drinking water brought pleasure. Two large, electrically driven pumps standing on the road to Loreta worked night and day to generate the town's main water supply, brought up from beneath the Vermejo to a huge, 800,000-gallon concrete reservoir on Capitan Hill, 140 feet above downtown. "Best damn stuff I ever tasted," says Babe Carlini.

Part of the fun of being a kid in Dawson was seeing what you could get away with. For George Dale, that meant sneaking into the Opera House to see a movie: "This was around 1930, and here's what we'd do. Somebody younger, maybe my brother Bill, or Coomy Jackovich, who lived up the street,

would pay the dime to get in and then go up in the balcony and open the fire escape door, and then a bunch of us would follow."

At any time of the year there was bound to be a shivaree. When someone got married in Dawson—say Matt Scanlon and Mary Lou Covert—the couple usually couldn't afford much of a honeymoon. Indeed, the wedding night often was spent in town at a friend's house. Every kid knew what house that was. At 3:00 A.M. after the wedding, youthful Dawsonites would go to that address, stand outside, and bang on pots and pans until the newlyweds came out and told the rabble-rousers to pipe down. If that didn't do the trick, and it usually didn't, the groom would reach down into his pockets for a bribe, usually a few coins or a candy bar.

Rich or poor, Greek or Mexican, growing up in Dawson meant lying in your bed at night and listening to the sounds outside: accordion music and wine-inspired singing and laughter, and footsteps on the street so familiar that you knew to whom those feet belonged. Growing up in Dawson meant dreaming. For Lena Colaizzi, the dream was to be an airline stewardess, though she'd seen only a couple of airplanes. For many young men, growing up meant thinking about your father coming home dog-tired and soot-covered from the mine. Would you follow him? You certainly wanted to work, for that was the Dawson way. For many in town, work became a chief means of coming of age. For Harmon Black, work meant delivering the *Denver Post*, a day late, around town for a nickel. On his route, Black usually would stop at the Snake, which at the time had a big painting of a nude woman hanging behind the bar. Wearing knickers and a newsboy cap, Black would walk in and try not to stare at that startling piece of art. At some point a miner usually would say to him, "Hey, Harmon, you can come in, but I don't want you to look at that girl," which, of course, only made him look harder.

Paul Brozovich found work in a place just as entertaining as the Snake. Brozovich's parents ran a boardinghouse up by Number One Camp. It was a hostelry filled with single miners, one of whom eventually ran off with Brozovich's teenage sister and the boardinghouse profits. Brozovich's first job was delivery boy. Pulling a red, Radio Flyer wagon, he would take wine and beer and bread and eggs from the boardinghouse up to nearby Coontown, the unfortunately named black community at the north end of Dawson. To Camp Number Three, where the shot firers and foremen lived, he'd take chickens and rabbits. And a couple of times a day Brozovich did something numerous Dawson kids did: he went looking for coal. "I got scrap coal and the other stuff that fell off the cars on the way to the tipple, and hauled it home. We didn't have to pay to heat our house that way. I used to put about two gunnysacks worth of coal in that wagon a day. Only trouble was, every year or so we'd have to get a new wagon."

Though Bill Federici lived in Colfax, just outside Dawson, he went to school in Dawson and did all the things Dawsonites did, such as make cigars out of hay and horse manure and actually puff on the creations. Federici's father ran the Colfax Pavilion, a popular dance hall, and an adjacent grocery store. Federici would help his father book bands, and when he turned fourteen he drove his father's delivery truck, a ton-and-a-half Dodge, black with a yellow stripe. Federici was so small he couldn't see over the truck's dashboard—so he sat on a pillow.

Steve Schulte also assisted his father, who was a baker in the Mercantile. Every morning at about 5:00 A.M., starting when he was eight or nine, Schulte would go to the third floor of the company store and help the old man fry and frost doughnuts and wrap bread, on a big workbench. Schulte would stay there until 8:00 A.M. when school started. Schulte was the envy of his crowd—who didn't like glazed doughnuts? As for pay, Schulte never told his friends how much he earned. "Every other Saturday," he says, "I would get a bottle of pop for my work."

The Toe Ticklers. That was the name of the Dawson dance band to which Bob McClary belonged. "We'd tie a bass drum on the baggage rack of a '34 sedan and play roadhouses—the Club Luna in Raton, and at Colfax, and weddings at Maxwell and dances up on Johnson Mesa, northeast of Raton. We got $120 a night, which for a six-piece band was pretty darn good. I played trumpet. I was seventeen, and I don't know how I got into some of those clubs. Maybe we played that wedding at Maxwell for free. But we got all you could drink."

Surely one of the most industrious kids in Dawson was Pete Trujillo. Trujillo was about six or seven when he had his first job offer. This was in the late 1920s, a time when famous people used to periodically stop in Dawson, on their way to a dude ranch up just over the Colorado line. Douglas Fairbanks was said to have passed through. And Mary Pickford and Ina Rae Hutton. All sorts of big bands, too. Many of these people would stay at the Dawson Hotel, the long, skinny, barracks-like building that stood near the entrance to town. It was outside that hotel where Trujillo and his boyhood friends—Tony Hernández, Blas Padilla, Lito Padilla, and Mike Martínez—used to hang around. "One day," says Trujillo, "I seen Clark Gable there with a bunch of his cronies.

The Opera House offered first-run picture shows every week.

We didn't have enough sense to ask for an autograph, except that one of the men, a horseman from Oklahoma, I guess, told me that he could make me into a jockey. I was real little then. Still am. But I was pretty solid; I was tough as boot nails. Everybody wanted to whip me, but I ended up whipping them.

"So this buddy of Clark Gable's said, 'Why don't you come back to Kentucky with me and I'll train you myself?' I told him, 'Go see my dad.' And so the guy went up there. My dad was a machinist and welder who repaired mine cars. He told the man no. I was really too young to understand. Heck, when you're in Dawson, you were removed. We used to prepare for a trip to Raton, only 35 miles away, for two weeks."

After that experience Trujillo stayed in town and started to earn money—with a fervor. First, he delivered milk for a dairy south of town. The driver drove a horse-drawn hearse, while Trujillo followed on foot. Ran is more like it. Then he had a shoeshine job. He'd go to the Snake on payday, when money

was sure to be tossed around by miners as well as local cowboys, who would tie their horses up out front and, on occasion, even ride those horses through the saloon's swinging front doors. When Trujillo was about ten, he started selling chewing gum door-to-door in Dawson. An outfit in Cincinnati would send him two or three boxes of gum on consignment, and little Pete would walk around town and try to hawk it. Then he sold shoes and clothes door-to-door from a mail-order catalog. He sold women's dresses and panties even. If he sold five suits, he'd get one free. "I was the best-dressed kid in town," he remarks.

Not everything was idyllic for a Dawson child, of course. Sickness, particularly the 1918 influenza epidemic, left scars on the impressionable. "People were dying so fast," says Amelia Lopez García. "We had several bachelors in our neighborhood, and Mother would cook pots of soup and have us go and feed them. I think she saved quite a few people because they got a little nourishment." The bodies were taken to the cemetery by mule-drawn wagons, and García says that, even today, she can remember seeing them go by. Across the river from town, near the ranch, stood the pesthouse, a brick building where many kids were sentenced to recuperate during the days of scarlet fever and other scourges.

And, of course, the mines were always there, threatening to disrupt the innocence of youth. "The greatest fear I ever had growing up," says Albert Rivera, "was hearing the whistle blow." The power plant whistle would be set off whenever there was a mine explosion, accident, or fatality. "We knew when the whistle went off that it spelled disaster. It scared me."

The sight of the old Dodge ambulance could be just as traumatic for a kid. A fast-moving ambulance, every Dawsonite knew, carried a dead person. A slow-moving ambulance meant the miner inside had only been injured. Paul Brozovich was playing outside one day when he saw the ambulance rumble by a creek near his house. It was moving slowly, but ... When the vehicle got closer, Brozovich looked inside and saw his father, a miner also named Paul Brozovich, in the front seat. Young Paul ran down and jumped on the running board to get a better look. His father, he learned, had been cutting coal when a piece of cable had come down and stuck him in the right eye. He would lose the eye, but not his life.

The whistle could mean a fire, too—one blow for each number of the camp where the fire was located. "I was in the fourth grade and looked out the window of Douglas School and heard the whistle at the same time," says Albert Rivera. "It was our house burning down! My brother Pantaleon had been playing with matches. The company gave us food and clothing, and people gave us things. That was one thing about Dawson: when there was a disaster, the entire town rallied around."

Some childhood memories hurt even now. Livia Montepara Mora was ten years old when her mother died. As the eldest of three children, Livia then had to take care of her two younger sisters and her father, Pietro Montepara, a timberman.

"We had no relatives in Dawson, and it was hard. We were left on our own. That's what I resent today. We lived on Four Hill, and we didn't have anything. We were three dirty, little ragamuffins, and I remember an English woman would chase us away from her children. She didn't want her kids playing with us. Oh, only the people from old Mexico gave us the time of day. They might show up at our house with a tortilla for us.

"I had to cook and clean, and I only got to go to the fourth grade. I taught myself to read and write. It was hard.

Then when I was twelve, my father married again. I thought we had it made, but I was so wrong. This was a woman twenty years older than my father, and it didn't work out at all. She resented the three of us, my sisters and me. She started hitting us kids, and once she beat me so bad I had to go to the hospital. They took us kids away from my father, and I went to Raton to live. Finally, my father divorced her, and we went back to live with him.

"Dawson is where I met my husband, and we've been married more than fifty years. But Dawson is also a place that has for me much pain."

A lack of money, as the Monteparas and others would readily admit, did hurt Dawsonites, particularly during the Great Depression. "The times were hard, no question," says Henry Reza. "There were strikes in the mines, and families went without. But the Depression also gave us Dawson kids a better appreciation for the value of something simple—such as digging for arrowheads." "There *were* pay cuts and layoffs," says Alberta McClary. "But I think children in other towns felt the Depression more. We got by in Dawson; the words we always used were 'make do.'"

Language for a Dawson immigrant presented problems, but many newly arrived children seemed to look upon speaking as an adventure. "I couldn't speak English when I got there in 1918," says Amelia García. "But I didn't mind because most of the children were having the same trouble. We were so many nationalities. Our neighbors were Louis Massaroni and his wife, Emma. Their children said "hurley" for *hurry*, so I figured I had learned one word."

Thirteen stands out as a memorable age, a benchmark age when the recollection of childhood and its attendant nicknames were sealed, when the responsibility of adulthood and its disappointments were only vaguely suggested. Diane Holdridge was thirteen when she left Dawson in 1947. She had been reared there, roller-skating the hours away on the town's few sidewalks. Her father, Chester Pool, had been the industrial arts teacher in high school, and, like a lot of migrating Dawsonites, the Pools wound up in Albuquerque. "Everything in Albuquerque seemed so different," says Holdridge. "So puny. The rooms in our Albuquerque house were tiny compared to Dawson. And everything seemed flat, compared to Dawson. But what I noticed most about Albuquerque was that people went *through* it. In Dawson, you entered and left the same way. There was no exit. I thought all towns were like that."

For Roger Scanlon, some good memories of being age thirteen in Dawson surfaced at a crucial time in his life, as a healing force. Scanlon was in the navy in 1951, serving off the coast of Korea, on the USS *Partridge*, a minesweeper. On February 3, the *Partridge* got hit by a mine. It was a wooden ship, and the explosion ripped through the vessel. The blast killed about half of the twenty-eight men on board, and Scanlon lost his right leg. "I was hospitalized in Oakland for about nine months," he says. "I remember lying there, knowing I was 100 percent disabled, and feeling sorry for myself. Then I start thinking about Dawson and growing up there. All the good times. That's what started making me better. We had a gang in Dawson—me, my brother Gene, Danny Moore, Billy Meikle. We played kick-the-can, and we used to go to the slag dump and take a piece of corrugated iron and ride it down the hill like a toboggan. We used to steal apples from the orchard. There was a woman named Herman, and she claimed we threw coal at her sheets on the clothesline and put holes in them. Well, we did. I was never much for studying. I failed the seventh grade. When I was in the sixth grade, I got in trouble with Hannah McGarvey, the principal of Central School. She whacked me with that rubber hose she had. I got about three or four whacks. Quincy Shaw, he broke some school windows, and he got a lot more whacks, too. We got it right at the top of the back of the leg. It was a wonderful life then, and it kept me alive."

Chapter Four

MINING

*"Every night I dream I'm loading
coal, and every morning
I wake up tired."*

—Abraham Trujillo

The best part of Marcos García's day surely comes at noon, when he finally gets a chance to sit down and open the tin, juglike canister he brings from home. In the top part of his lunch bucket, García finds two salami sandwiches and an apple, while the bottom part serves as his water pail, big enough to hold nearly a gallon of liquid. There in the half-light, García's face is covered with soot and his body has been aching ever since he climbed out of bed at 4:30 A.M.; there a mile beneath the earth, the simplest food never tasted so good.

For those like Marcos García, who worked underground, or inside, as it was called, a day in Dawson really started on the man-trip, the little slow-moving train pulled by the miniature locomotive known as ''The Dinky,'' that took miners up the hill from town and back. The first stop was the lamp house, where you picked up a battery-powered helmet lamp that had been recharged overnight. You also were handed a brass check, a round disk marked with a number—Number 426 if you were Marcos García—from a board on the wall, and you clipped it to your belt. At the end of the day, when the guardian of the lamp house was sure no one was in the mines, when he had all his lamps back and all the brass checks had been returned to the board, the shots, or explosive charges, could be fired. Failure to ''check out'' caused a messenger to be sent to your home, and perhaps even a search of the mine. In addition, it could mean a fine anywhere between a $1.50 and $25.00.

Also at the lamp house you were given ten to twenty other checks, metal disks this time. These had the same number as your brass tag, and they went into the pocket of your bib overalls. Inside the mine, you snapped one of these checks onto a loaded coal car, to get credit for your work, for the number also appeared on your pay slip. The metal checks had one more function, but no one talked about it much: in case of a cave-in or explosion they might be used to identify you.

With lunch bucket, helmet, and checks in tow, it was time to go inside and, if you were lucky, to the *buen terreno*, the best spot to work. One of the first things that you always noticed, no matter how many years you had been underground, was the cold. Even on Dawson's warmest summer days you could see your breath in the mine. Giant fans, brought in to settle the coal dust, made things colder still, even for those who wore heavy sheepskin coats and rubber boots. "By the time you rode into the mine a few miles," says Abe Trujillo, "your feet would be frozen."

After you inspected the ceiling at your work area and set your props, or supports, you sprinkled down the face you were digging; then you began to load coal into cars, and sometimes, as Marcos García says, "You put your back in there too."

Coal mining in Dawson utilized the room-and-pillar method, which meant digging a series of entries into the bed. From there, rooms—some almost as big as a football field—were cut, divided by huge pillars, which were part of the mine itself. Each room was mined, and then the pillars, nearly as large as the rooms themselves, were cleared, or pulled, upon

leaving, though this didn't often happen in Dawson.

For many years the inside work in Stag Cañon's mines was done by pick and shovel. Mechanization began arriving in the late 1920s, initially with cutting and scraping machines and belt conveyors that replaced loading by hand. Who worked underground? Many more men than worked aboveground, or outside. There were the miners, of course, who, in addition to digging, once tamped in their own explosives; and the shot firers who set those charges; and the fire bosses, who checked for gas and the conditions of the face. There also were loaders and haulers and timberers and tracklayers and sprinklers and strangely named subspecialists, such as nippers, who operated the coal elevators; and trapper boys, who opened trapdoors to another section; and bratticemen, who worked the ventilation system; and spraggers, who set the props in the roof of a mine.

Mules once trudged coal out of Dawson's mines. "I used to get so mad at the mules I wanted to kill 'em," says Mike Faba, who started working in Dawson in 1913. "But you couldn't kill a mule. You could kill a man in Dawson then, but you couldn't kill a mule. You got fired." When machines took over for the animals, in came shuttle cars—long trains steered by motormen seated at the rear. The coal in these cars went first to the tipple, where each car was unloaded and then its contents sorted. Using one of the first hydro-separators, a screening process that automatically isolated pure coal from ash-forming impurities, Dawson established a reputation for turning out the cleanest coal around. Dawson, in fact, turned out four types of clean coal. From biggest to smallest, the varieties were: Fancy Lump, Fancy Egg, Fancy Nut, and Fancy Pea. Adjacent to the tipple were the crushing house and the washer, where the coal was smoothed and

With lunch pail and pick, a Dawson miner
was ready for a day's work.

bathed before being placed on conveyor belts that traveled to waiting railroad cars. Outside workers ranged from tipple and washery men to blacksmiths and dumpers, firemen and engineers, and carpenters and electricians, some of whom worked at the power plant, the supporting station that ultimately replaced a barn full of mules.

Noise and the darkness limited much talking underground. In fact, many miners learned to communicate with the lights on their helmets. A nod meant a motorman should come forward. Shaking your head back and forth indicated a coal car was full. Turning your head back and around told the motorman to go in reverse. When they could hear each other, usually sitting with a lunch bucket between their legs, the water pail often spiked with honey for energy, miners talked most often of sports or women. They saved mining—"hollowing out them hills"—as a topic for the bars, where, oddly enough, women weren't found until Dawson's final decade.

If saloon talk was about coal, it probably wasn't about Dawson's coal belonging to the Vermejo formation of the upper Cretaceous geological system, a 100-million-year-old field that pocked northeastern New Mexico. The Dawson mines were located upon the lower of two workable seams, known as the Blossburg or Raton seam. The coal lay almost horizontal, which made it easier to excavate, for no hoisting was necessary.

When fifty men went to work in the Dawson Fuel Company's first year of operation, 1901, the community's sole mine produced 300 tons of coal. Production increased significantly after the first car load of coal passed over the newly constructed tipple on May 22, 1902. When Phelps Dodge arrived in 1905 and set up the Stag Cañon Fuel Company, its branch operation, suddenly there was more coal than *anyone*

had imagined. By 1906, a labor force of 1,539 worked six Dawson mines, and more than 100 coke ovens burned like eternal flames. The growth was staggering: three years later, more than 1 million tons of coal were being pulled from the ground, making the Dawson operation second in coal production in New Mexico, just behind the sprawling operation of St. Louis, Rocky Mountain and Pacific Company, in such towns as Brilliant, Gardiner, Van Houten, Koehler, and Sugarite.

With so much demand for coal and coke, there was nothing holding back Dawson. By 1921, approximately 32,000 of the town's 50,000 acres were used for mining one-third of the state's coal. Seventy miles of track wormed in and out of ten mines, while the deepest pit sat two and a half miles down. The coke operation increased to more than 500 ovens that produced 600 tons per day.

What could an inside man make? Records from 1909 reveal a shot firer pulled down $3.25 a day, a good wage, but out of that had to come $2.75 for a keg of powder, which might last a few weeks. A pit boss earned $125 a month, also decent, though deductions included lamp oil, which ran $.70 a gallon. Tony Arcangeli remembers earning $600 to $700 a year. For many years miners were paid by what they dug: contract work, it was called. Outside, a company checkweighman would inspect the scales to see how much each car—with metal check attached—weighed, and a miner was paid accordingly, minus any dirty coal found. Thus, a car holding 3,000 pounds of coal might be found by a checkweighman to hold only 1,500 pounds. It wasn't a terribly accurate system and often caused great dissension in Dawson. "You heard that song about sixteen tons?" asks Margarito Martínez. "Sixteen tons of coal ain't nothing. I loaded as much as fifty tons a day."

Jitters abounded on a new miner's first day. "I was so nervous," says Al Schulte, "that I thought about jumping off the man-trip and never going back. The next day I was okay." A new miner often found himself under the sixty-forty system. That is, 60 percent of his profits went to the man who was breaking him in. Al Schulte's mentor was Joe Tennant. "My pick didn't mean much. When I hit it, it bounced back. Old Joe, he showed me how to do it. I worked under him for six months, and later on I went to a scraper." As a scraperman, Marcos García made $200 for a "half," or fifteen days. During the Depression, when miners only worked a few days each week, Bob Lucero cleared, at most, $3.00 a day digging coal under contract, $.90 a ton. Chon Viramontes always did "company work," and so was paid by his time, at the most, $1.00 an hour. In 1940, a miner's income averaged around $50.00 a month. But out of that came deductions—for rent, coal fuel, medical, powder and fuses, lamps—that left him with about $25.00. Thus, he'd often draw scrip—credit against future wages and issued in paper and coins—from the company store. Things had improved some by the late 1940s: Dave Córdova was making $13.60 a day digging coal, and Chuy Ponce took home $2.00 an hour as a shuttle car operator. Nobody got wealthy in Dawson, but, when the mines were operating, work was steady. Many miners, particularly during Dawson's boom years of the 1920s, regularly bought new cars. In 1928, for instance, it was estimated that 85 percent of the community's work force owned automobiles.

Young men in Dawson, eager to earn a wage, frequently would lie to get inside the mines. At age fifteen, Abe Trujillo told the corporation that he was eighteen. He wanted inside because his father, Max, was undergound, doing pick and shovel work, and Abe felt he should be with him. "When

A familiar sight at the mines: shuttle cars pulling coal.

you're a miner's son," says Dave Córdova, "the thing to do is to follow the old man's tracks." Córdova had quit high school to serve in the army, and when he returned to Dawson at age nineteen, his father, Manuel, told him, "Now that you're back in town, let's get you a job in the mine." "I said, 'Okay,'" says Córdova. "I didn't know no better." The day after he graduated from high school, Margarito Martínez went "straight to the hole," where he joined his father, Felix, a Dawson miner since 1915.

Working alongside your father was sometimes an eye-opening experience. Arthur "Stach" DiLorenzo quit school his senior year to join his father, Dominic, in Mine Number Six. "At first I couldn't stand him. He wouldn't let you stop. These were the hand drill days, before electric drills, and it was hard. I finally could load more than him, and that's when we got along." When Fred Cericola was a sophomore in high school, his father Jay, a mine foreman, took him underground. "I stayed all day and saw all I needed to see," says Fred. "I knew I never wanted to work there." Nor did Mike Faba. "I dug coal for about a month," he says, "but I hated it. I didn't put it there, so why should I take it out?"

While numerous fathers in Dawson encouraged their offspring to follow them into the mines, many fathers did the opposite. Clemente Di Domenico, a car-dropper, an outside man, repeatedly told his sons he didn't want them underground because "I don't want a roof of coal to come down on your heads." Domenic Salvo had sneaked into the mines at age twelve to work, loved his job, and hardly missed a day in thirty years. But Salvo didn't want that for his sons. "Dad used to brag about graduating from junior high," says his son, Sam. "But actually he wanted us to go on to college. He saw the shortcomings of the mines." Sam eventually spent a year working at the tipple, but finally quit and went to college when he grew tired of hearing his father hound him to do just that.

Inside or outside the mines, one sound could be heard more than any other in Dawson: coughing. Just about everybody who had gone underground for any length of time coughed, particularly those miners who had worked in the first twenty-five years of the town's life, when coal dust wasn't sprayed and ventilation was poor. Because so many people coughed, even slightly, nobody paid much attention. Certainly not Abe Trujillo, who worked inside for almost a quarter of a century. Only after Trujillo came to Albuquerque to live in the late 1950s did his coughing increase and he decide to seek help. A bronchoscopy showed he had pneumoconiosis, or black lung disease, the irreversible presence of coal dust in the lungs.

"Back there in Dawson," says Trujillo, "nobody said much about black lung. Nobody knew what it was." Trujillo now has trouble breathing; he can no longer exercise and even gets tired walking. But he considers himself one of the lucky ones, along with his father who worked more than thirty years but never showed a sign of sickness, other than a cough. "Nick Grano, a guy I worked with in Dawson, he got black lung," says Trujillo. "He got it so bad he couldn't wash his face without oxygen. He couldn't shave without oxygen. Nick finally died. He choked to death."

Rooney Wiggins had worked on and off in Dawson's mines for fifteen years, starting as a pick and shovel man, and he began to get sick in the late 1970s. "For about ten years, he was on oxygen," says Vernice Smock Wiggins, the woman Rooney met and married in Dawson. "Rooney had worked a long time in the mines when they weren't ventilated, and it had finally caught up with him." Wiggins died in the Miner's Hospital in Raton in 1990, the day before he would have turned eighty-three. "Rooney wasn't angry at the end, and I wasn't either," says his widow. "You accepted life the way it was in Dawson, the good and the bad."

Black lung, which first shows up as silicosis, a nodular disease, was such a part of life in Dawson that one rarely saw elderly miners in town: if a miner did retire there, the steep hills kept him from getting around much. When an old underground man died in Dawson, death was often attributed to "miner's disease."

When Felix Martínez died in 1949, medical records say the cause of death was an appendicitis. Martínez's children say the veteran Dawson miner, then sixty-two, simply could no longer breathe.

Though black lung was not yet medically identified, some Dawsonites seemed to understand how to deal with it. All the

Before Dawson's mines became mechanized,
mules did a lot of the dirty work.

while he worked as a miner, Abe Trujillo refused to smoke, and he thinks that helped his lung problem remain mild for many years. Chon Viramontes, who went to work in the mines at age sixteen, never smoked or took a drink in his life. As he nears age eighty, Viramontes swears that's the reason his lungs are clear. Then there were the home remedies used to ward off potential lung ailments. Italian miners preferred long, thin black cigars: aboveground they puffed them; underground they chewed them. Indeed, many Dawson miners believed that chewing tobacco kept their lungs free from coal dust, certainly more so than chewing gum. If you chewed gum underground, one theory went, you'd swallow the dust. If you chewed tobacco, you'd spit it out. Marcos García, who worked twenty-seven years as a Dawson miner, confirms this theory: García stuck a plug of Day's Work in his mouth every morning, and he now goes dancing a couple of times a week —at age ninety. Chuy Ponce says the first time he chewed tobacco he got nauseous and vomited. "But you learned. There were some tough guys in there who could take a plug of Day's Work and stick it into their cheek, then put a hunk of Beechnut on their tongue, and then slip some snuff between their gums. Three different things in the mouth at one time."

Many Dawson miners took care of themselves by adhering to superstitions. In Dawson's early days, blacks, thought to be ill-boding, were not particularly welcome in the mines, a message underscored by the *Raton Range*. In a September 1903 article detailing a mine explosion in Dawson, the newspaper listed the three dead as: "Serapio Ragel, Miguel Salazar and a negro." When Phelps Dodge gained control, discrimination ceased to exist. However, P.D. never permitted women to work underground. In Dawson and other coalfields in the country, letting a woman anywhere near a mine surely would bring a run of misfortune. In fact, every time a mine blew up in Dawson, people in town wondered if a woman had been inside. That women inside a coal mine could bring bad luck is truly an American phenomenon, since women had worked alongside men in British and eastern European mines. But in Dawson it was *verboten*. Even such a tragedy as a stillborn was at times attributed to women going underground.

Certain beliefs and customs came about with good reason. Once upon a time, particularly after an explosion, Dawson miners carried with them underground a canary in a cage. If the bird became asphyxiated and ceased singing, the miners quickly left, for the dead animal indicated the presence of carbon monoxide, produced by any blast in an unventilated area. Miners occasionally kept mice or rats underground, and fed them during breaks. If one of those pet rodents was spotted trying to leave, it revealed that trouble, likely in the form of methane gas, lay ahead. Methane is constantly given off in most coal mines and forms an explosive mixture with air. For many years the gas generally was believed to be almost wholly responsible for mine explosions. Eventually, miners used a special lamp to detect methane. If the gas was present, the flame in the lamp would rise and fall, a sure signal to exit the mine.

Though most Catholics who went underground made the sign of the cross before entering a mine, Dawson miners still suffered their share of accidents. After all, coal mining, even under the most ideal conditions, is hazardous, and few people who worked the town's mines were not touched by some calamity. Simply, accidents were part of Dawson's daily existence. "The coal will warn you when it will burst," says Margarito Martínez. "It sounds like popcorn." Adds

Matt Valdez: "The mountain talks to you. When you hear a rumble, you know where it is and you got to listen. You throw down your tools and you get out." Valdez was once buried for three hours in Mine Number Six. "We were working at the entry, and there was a rumble. A prop broke and hit me in the back and knocked me out. This was about 1938 or so. They managed to get me out. Some of the timbers were so low that, riding on the motor, you had to duck low. One motorman got killed because he didn't duck enough. Squashed his head."

Dawson's miners were forever testing the roof of a mine with a pick. A hollow sound was not a good omen. Later, roofs in the mines were bolted—never with thirteen bolts, however—just as coal cars were soaked with water and floors sprinkled, or "mudited," with adobe, to keep down the dust and avoid the possibility of an explosion. Even with these precautions there always existed the fear of an accident—a timber snapping, a rib rolling, a rock falling. Some accidents left mental scars. Henry Reza was putting in dummies when he saw something he would never forget. "Dummies are long sacks, like sausages, filled with sand. You put the powder and cap in a hole first for blasting, and then you ram the dummies in behind the powder. It keeps the blast all in one place. A car filled with those dummies one day ran over a man who worked near me. Joe Profilio. He'd been in the mines forty years and was on his last day. The car jumped the track and ran right over his face. I was only about twenty at the time, and it was hard to take."

Other accidents left physical scars. "I was working as a mine foreman, and we were shorthanded, since this was the war," says Stach DiLorenzo. "I'd done this a thousand times: pick up loaded cars and give them a load of empties. This time,

For Dawson's first twenty-five years, the coke ovens burned brightly.

I don't know what made this trip keep going. Maybe the brakes went out. There was brushing on the ground, which made it rough to walk. Anyway, I stumbled and fell, and coal cars went over my left hand. Ran over it twice. I could hear it: a loud bang. I picked myself up and looked down at my hand. I had a glove on, and so I pulled it off. Right then I saw how bad it was. I saw it was crushed.

"The doctor came down from Raton, and they talked about it in the hospital there in Dawson, but in the end they decided to take my hand off above the wrist. Today, they'd probably try to save it. I got really sick when they told me. Mostly I got mad at myself because it shouldn't have happened. The company sent me to Kansas City to get fitted with an artificial hook, and I still use it today. It helps that I'm right-handed."

Though Phelps Dodge took the blame for DiLorenzo's misfortune, a large percentage of accidents in Dawson, P.D. claimed, was due to carelessness and probably could have been prevented if proper safety measures had been followed.

Cleaning and sorting coal took place at the washery.

As far back as 1912, this seemed to be the case when a miner named John Toya was killed in Mine Number Four. Phelps Dodge's report on the death said: "The deceased was in a neighboring room from his own workplace in the mine and was sitting and conversing with the workmen in that room when a large rock fell on him." The state mine inspector, final judge for fatalities, agreed with P.D., as he usually did. "The deceased should have been in his own working place," the inspector wrote. Shot firers were continually at risk. On April 15, 1920, five shot firers in Dawson died in Mine Number Six. The five were the only men in the mine at the time, and their deaths followed the detonation of explosives. The official explanation, submitted by P.D. and accepted by the state mine inspector, said, "The five apparently reentered the mine contrary to the rules of the company." Of Joe Profilio, the sixty-four-year-old shot firer that Henry Reza saw crushed by a locomotive, P.D. filed this report: "Had Profilio stayed in the wooden car, he would have been safe." That accident

and many others were classified "1E," meaning the fault lay with the injured employee. Timberman Fernando Contreras was killed on January 21, 1949, while repairing a roof. Normally, P.D. would have reported this accident as a "9C," blaming the roof collapse for the death. But the company's report, filed with the state mine inspector, says, "If he (Contreras) stood still, he would not have been injured."

If these responses seem unsympathetic, Phelps Dodge merely was trying to protect itself, while at the same time protect its employees, for numerous accidents *were* due to recklessness. On occasion, a Dawsonite fought an official ruling that claimed he had been negligent. In 1915, three Greek miners hired famed Raton attorney Henry Kiker to file a lawsuit against the Stag Cañon Fuel Company over injuries they said occurred due to the company's negligence. Many of these lawsuits were settled out of court, for Phelps Dodge did not want bad publicity. Most of the time, however, workers accepted the fact that getting injured was part of the job. And P.D. helped workers accept this by continually reminding them that, if safety measures were followed correctly, no injuries would occur.

Safety had been preached before the terrible 1913 explosion, but most of the sermons unfortunately came afterward. Following nine fatal accidents in 1914, a "Safety First" department was organized, said P.D.'s annual report that year, to "remedy this evil and replace the present voluntary method." When new electric locomotives arrived in 1915, a warning light system was installed. A red light was hung beside each white mine light, and when a trip of cars passed one light, the next would automatically light to give advanced warning. A safety committee, made up of working men and executive staff, was formed, and it made regular inspection tours of the mines. A practical mining school also was started, whereby a new miner would spend seventy days working in the entry of a mine. Safety became the war cry of the *Dawson News*. In 1921, these pieces of advice appeared in the weekly newspaper:

- "Don't abuse a mule; push on the car and help him; he is helping you."
- "Don't put the small end of a timber up; put the big end up."
- "Thou shall not steal thy brother's wedge."

First-aid classes in applying bandages and splints were held at the Rescue Station on Church Row, a combination practice mine, lecture hall, and technical library burrowed into the side of Capitan Hill. There, in a $6,620 facility modeled on a similar center in Nova Scotia, compulsory lectures were given twice a week to everyone, including the company chemist. Certificates of competency ranged from knowledge of gases to use of gas masks. To simulate underground conditions, instructors pumped formaldehyde fumes into the make-believe mine. At one point classes were held on different nights for those speaking different languages. In 1924, the Spanish class had 284 members, the Italian had 155, the Slavic 65, the Greek 23, and the English-speaking class 195. Supplementing these seminars twice a year representatives from the United States Bureau of Mines visited Dawson to give first-aid instruction. Even the state mine inspector participated: he often spent as long as a week in Dawson, attending lectures, going on work crews, and just observing.

First-aid team competition that offered cash prizes and trophies to be kept on display in a mine were held periodically, with the winners advancing to regional tournaments. A Dawson team once placed seventeenth out of sixty-three teams

In Dawson, great emphasis was placed on safety and mine rescue.

at the International First-Aid and Mine Rescue Contest in Salt Lake City. Competition wasn't necessarily for the young men, either. One year Dawson claimed the oldest first-aid team in America—six men with a combined total age of 360 years.

While preventing loss of life was of utmost importance to Phelps Dodge, the company's goal was to prevent any injury, no matter how small. During the first four months of 1921, for example, twenty-nine nonfatal accidents took place in Dawson's mines. To reduce that alarming number, P.D. posted such signs as "Is That Prop Too Close to Track?" or "Be Careful of Your Eyes," across the sides of every pit car. For a while following the 1923 mine explosion, men were searched for matches before going underground. "If found, he's careless and thoughtless," went the slogan. In 1928, men weren't allowed to go *anywhere* without hard hats, goggles, and safety shoes.

*Even with a cutting machine, nobody said
coal mining was easy.*

Time lost to accidents meant time lost to production and thus money lost. Not surprisingly, some accidents occurred because of that rush for production. More than one foreman in Dawson told his crew to race their shuttle cars in order to fill as many cars as possible in the shortest time. "We'd have a beer party if we finished first," says Dave Córdova. And yet, even with that sort of pressure, safety was stressed. For many years, the mine with the best record based on tonnage of coal produced and the fewest number of days lost on account of accidents got to stretch a banner above its portal.

No one escaped the emphasis placed on safety. Miners' families were awarded free movie passes if no accidents occurred. Kids were encouraged to enter mine safety poster contests. Wives were told to warn husbands not to put tobacco juice over a cut and bind the wound with a rag, lest it become infected. And if anyone needed further reminders, the *Dawson News* ran periodic editorials, such as: "Safety First is your friend. It insures you a full set of ten fingers and ten toes at-tached to a sound body free from wounds and infirmities."

Injured men were encouraged, subconsciously perhaps, to go back to work as soon as possible, particularly in the days when the union wasn't strong in Dawson and workmen's compensation meant nothing. Mike Faba worked as a nipper when a coal car crushed his finger in 1917. "I didn't go to the doctor. If you went to the doctor, you got fired. It swelled up, and I put two sticks on it at home." Only three weeks after doctors amputated his left hand, Stach DiLorenzo returned underground. Although coal fell on Bruno Bergamo's head and caused him to be hospitalized, he was back on the job the following day, with an open gash in his skull. Going back to work quickly was economical. "Sure, miners were afraid after the explosions," says Margarito Martínez, who dug coal in Dawson for twenty years. "But you got to eat." Hurrying back to the mines after an accident was also a matter of pride. A cave-in shattered Kelly Mora's jaw and face; a month later he had returned to running a loader, even though his supervisor advised him against it. "I didn't want to be afraid of that mine," Mora says. Attempting to stop a runaway train of coal cars, Charlie Mataya broke the instep of his foot. "I went in the next day wearing a cast," he says. "Why? Mostly because I was a damn fool. The company was always striving for a safety record; they wouldn't push you if you didn't want to work. The doc said to me, 'You're going to be off work six weeks!' I said, 'No, I'm going back.' I didn't give a damn about the safety record. I was a miner and that was that."

Accidents led Dawson miners to help one another, and job level or ethnic background mattered little at those times. John McCarty was a broad-shouldered fire boss, the man responsible for checking leaks and creaks in the mine, and then carving his initials in the face when he had finished. The day falling rock pinned McCarty underground, his rescuer was an ordinary Slavic laborer, a little fellow, who risked his life to pull the rubble away and then carry McCarty safely outside. Crews elsewhere might have resented McCarty's authority, but not in Dawson. When one of their own was killed, Dawson miners banded together in ritual: they walked slowly with each other to the town cemetery to lay their coworker to rest, facing west, often beneath a headstone bearing the design of a crossed pick and shovel.

According to the state mine inspector's records, Jay Cericola, who died August 8, 1949, became the final mine fatality in the town. At age forty-eight, Cericola was the foreman of Mine Number Six when falling rock killed him. It was a sad day in the community, for Cericola had worked on and off in the mines since 1916. Born in Italy, he had come to Dawson when he was three years old. Cericola knew the dangers of mining well; his father John lay facing west in the town cemetery, a victim of Dawson's 1913 explosion. Jay Cericola was not only a popular man in town, but his son, Fred, about to be a senior at Dawson High School, was a good student and a fine athlete.

Jay Cericola had been giving timbering instructions to Pete Montoya, who was driving a joy loader nearby. When an arm of Montoya's loader hooked a crossbar supporting the roof, the ceiling came down. Though Fred Cericola calls his father's death an accident, the official version suggests otherwise. State mine inspector records say that Montoya should have used a hand shovel rather than a loader to pick up loose coal. When an emotional Montoya argued his case at a hearing, state mine inspector John García replied, "We are not trying to convict you of murder, Pete."

Mine safety was not all that concerned Phelps Dodge. P.D.'s history had been marked by some celebrated labor disputes, and the corporation was determined that would not happen at the Stag Cañon Branch. In Bisbee, Arizona, in 1917, union activity caused Phelps Dodge to ship more than 1,100 workers out of that copper town in cattle cars. Because of labor strikes in Colorado two years later, National Guard troops came to Dawson to keep an eye on things.

Dawson had always been a peaceful place, and Phelps Dodge wanted it to remain so. As far back as 1906, the company had dealt with suspected strikers and agitators by putting them on the Maxwell stage line. A company official told the *Raton Daily Range*, "This keeps camp quiet and makes a good living place for the working men." There were early stirrings in town of the Western Federation of Miners and the International Workers of the World, but the two labor organizations had much better success in other states, such as Arizona and Colorado. In fact, between 1893 and 1919 such labor-management relations that set off violent "mining wars" were almost nonexistent in New Mexico. In Phelps Dodge's 1918 annual report, T. H. O'Brien, the general manager of the Stag Cañon Branch, wrote, "There was absolutely no labor unrest of any kind at Dawson during the year, and the same friendly feeling exists between employees and the company that has prevailed for several years." But as Dawson prospered—between P.D.'s arrival in 1905, and 1920, seven new mines opened, and the community became the biggest single producer of coal in the Southwest—Phelps Dodge began to worry.

There was some reason to worry. Reportedly, Mary Harris Jones, the celebrated American labor agitator known as "Mother Jones," had planned a visit to Dawson in 1913, until business called her elsewhere. The following year, the United Mine Workers of America tried to organize workers of the Rockefeller-owned Colorado Fuel and Iron Company. When organizers and strikers were deported to New Mexico, violence erupted, culminating in the famed "Ludlow Massacre." On Easter night in 1914, twelve children, two women, and ten men were killed in a gun battle between miners and militiamen in Ludlow, Colorado, only about fifty miles north of Dawson.

By 1924, Dawson had grown to the largest town in the Southwest supported by a single industry, and the great number of immigrants arriving, the Red Scare that was sweeping the country, and the rise of John L. Lewis's United Mine Workers of America caused Phelps Dodge to take precautions. Even though Dawson was located in an inaccessible and isolated canyon at the end of a railroad line, P.D. became suspicious of any newcomers who might be potential troublemakers and anarchists. Such people were checked every time a train pulled in, and the town marshal, employed by Phelps Dodge, had the power to "kick down the canyon" any undesirable. Mail was inspected and goods not purchased by scrip or through the company store often were sent back. Dawson, after all, was too important a source of coal and coke for P.D. to be unconcerned.

Much of Phelps Dodge's action toward possible disruption came in the form of a psychological strategy, a corporate kindness that historian Richard Melzer termed "welfare capitalism." Give the miners and their families a decent lifestyle, tell them how good they have it, and they will be less inclined to cause trouble. Chief conveyor of this message of contentment and goodwill was the town's newspaper, published by Phelps Dodge's Welfare Department. While the *Dawson News* pro-moted the town in every way possible, it also was used to quell any impending disorder in the ranks. The *DN* wrote that a "true citizen" was akin to a "loyal patriot" who backed the company without question. The newspaper urged readers not to criticize the company, but rather "you should only look at yourself." And the paper continually reminded Dawsonites about how good things were, even as many miners struggled to make ends meet. "There were nine children in our family," says Josephine Marcelli Andazola, "and when my father used to come home from the mines, we would go to his lunch bucket and see if he left us anything, you know, part of a sandwich, a piece of fruit." Never mind, proclaimed the *Dawson News*: "Compare your position with those who are less fortunate than yourself."

P.D. established a Welfare Committee in 1921 to open communication channels between the working men and executives. The committee, a sort of controlled union, was in a sense formed to prevent what miners saw as injustices, such as the checkweighman system. But the Welfare Committee had little influence, and certainly no power to lobby for better pay, a goal in 1922. Nationwide coal reductions that year had caused Phelps Dodge to cut earnings for a ten-hour day from $7.60 to $5.25 and to place many employees on a three-day work week. A group of miners, led by John "Rabbit" Smith, protested the actions to the company. When P.D. ignored their grievances, the miners went on strike, the first *huelga* in Dawson history. In reaction, company recruiters traveled to Mexico and brought back replacements for the striking miners. Finally, on September 5, 1922, P.D. restored the better pay scale but "kicked down the canyon" Smith and other striking miners.

Short-lived strikes took place in the years that followed, and

Dawson fueled railroads and depended on them to transport its coal.

in 1927 more labor problems in Colorado coal mines caused thirty National Guard troops to be placed in Dawson to watch for potential IWW agitators, a deployment applauded by the town newspaper. A year later, the *DN* encouraged workers to vote Republican. When miner Sylver Lorenzo announced he would not and was subsequently fired after the election, along with seventy other men, a small riot broke out—windows were broken, buildings overturned—that the *DN* blamed on "vandals." A walkout in 1930 caused the company to threaten Felix Martínez with eviction. "Do you want your children to starve?" a P.D. official asked the miner. "Well," said Martínez, who worked ten hours a day for only a few dollars, "my twelve kids have gone hungry for years."

The Depression sparked big changes in Dawson's labor movement. Miners who had been hesitant about organizing before now faced a bleak economy—Dawson soon had only one mine running—and so began to feel differently. Mickie Mollica, a UMWA organizer, was suddenly welcomed by workers as was Martha Roberts, a radical labor leader. But the National Industrial Recovery Act, passed by Congress in June 1933, acted as the big push Dawson miners needed. The NIRA guaranteed laborers the right to unionize, bargain collectively, and to obtain better working conditions. Soon, Telesfor "Pee Wee" Gallegos and Danny Jones, a black miner, began rallying their fellow workers in Dawson through speeches and petitions to form a UMWA local. Tony Montoya, Tony Trujillo, Jenny Milano, and the rehired Sylver Lorenzo aided the recruitment effort. In August 1933, UMWA Local 6419 received a charter, and members named Gallegos as president, Jones, vice president, and Pete Milano, treasurer. Ninety-five percent of the miners in Dawson paid $1.40 a month for dues, with approximately a third of that sum going to the national office, a third to the District Fifteen office, and a third to the local office.

Phelps Dodge, however, refused to recognize the local. Thus, meetings were held that summer in secret, five miles down the road at the Colfax Pavilion. Chief topics at the gatherings were: the checkweighman system and better wages. Dawson miners still did not have their own checkweighman, and pay had dropped from $4.70 a day to $4.44. On October 1, 1933, Pee Wee Gallegos entered Mine Number Six and immediately turned over his water pail, the traditional signal for a wildcat strike.

That walkout lasted nearly a month. Toward the end of it, Gilbert O. Davis, the Stag Cañon Branch manager, announced that P.D. was going to close the one mine operating in town. On October 31, striking miners returned to find their own checkweighman system in place and better pay, though still no union recognition. Had P.D. given in? No, for not long afterward the company fired Gallegos and Jones. A public meeting was held in the Opera House, but the company held firm.

Dawson was not the only New Mexico town experiencing labor problems at this time. Across the state, coal miners in Gallup had gone on strike in 1933, and on April 4, 1935, labor agitation in that city caused eight shootings and left three men dead.

Local 6419 would not resort to violence, but it continued to be active, and in 1936 Dawson miners again went on strike. This time Phelps Dodge refused to open the company store to strikers. Narciso Federici, a Colfax grocer in whose pavilion the miners had been meeting, stepped in to offer his own goods for sale.

Eventually, Dawson's rank and file began meeting in the town gymnasium instead of at Colfax, for John L. Lewis's United Mine Workers of America organization was rapidly gaining wide acceptance. But, despite their boldness, Dawson local members still had to pay their monthly dues, still had to "check off," out of their own pockets. Phelps Dodge simply continued to refuse to acknowledge the union's existence.

A nationwide fifty-four day coal strike in 1943 changed things forever in Dawson. On November 4, 1943, after years of disappointment and anguish, the company finally accepted Local 6419 as the legal bargaining agent for Dawson miners. In early 1945, Stag Cañon's new manager, G. O. Arnold, signed a UMWA contract, and for the first time Dawson became a closed shop, whose members now paid monthly dues of $3.50. "Once the company recognized the union," says Charlie Mataya, recording secretary for Local 6419 for several years, "things started to happen." Most notable among them were portal-to-portal pay and retirement benefits.

Mining coal in Dawson was like tieing shoelaces: you simply didn't think much about it. "Did I like it?" asks Chuy Ponce. "Well, I got worked six and a half hours and got paid for eight. But I never saw the sun on weekdays. You went in when it was dark, and you came out when it was dark. I guess it was a good experience, but I wouldn't do it again."

Marcos García would go back. "I loved working the mines, going in there in the pitch-dark with your lunch bucket, working with people who depended on you, your partners. I loved turning off my lamp and listening to the twisting and the turning. I started in Dawson in 1923 and worked till 1950. I started with a pick and ended with a continuous mining machine that cuts coal. I had a great time. When I started there were ten mines and almost 2,000 miners, and when I stopped there was one mine and eighty-seven miners. People can't believe I survived all that time, that I'm ninety and don't even wear no eyeglasses. Why did I survive? My mother always told me 'Marcos, wherever you go, God will take care of you.' And He has."

Chapter Five

DYING

"You always lived in fear."
—Katherine McCarty Dale

Hazel Henry lay in bed on the second floor of the Dawson Hospital and wondered when she would be going home. The week before, Hazel had delivered a healthy boy, Tom Henry, Jr., and since then she had grown increasingly restless.

Hazel's window faced Dawson's Main Street, and all Hazel heard that Wednesday afternoon, October 22, 1913, was the clop clop clop of horses outside, and every now and then the sound of Frank Diver's Oakland or Tom O'Brien's Cadillac or the little runabout driven by Doc Evans, three of the perhaps half-dozen motorcars in the town of 3,100 people.

The warm and pleasant air coming in her window caused Hazel to drift off to sleep. Finally, sometime in the mid-afternoon, Hazel wakened to see a nurse enter the room. "We're going to be needing your bed," the nurse said. *Good*, Hazel thought, *at last I'm going to be discharged*. But the nurse's face had a strangely dark expression. "Up at the mines," she said, "there's been a terrible accident."

A terrible accident. It's probably safe to say that three words never carried so much weight.

Two miles from where Hazel lay her uncle, T. H. O'Brien, sat in the Stag Cañon Fuel Company's mine office and studied papers in front of him. With four mines working full shifts, it had been a typically busy day for the general manager. Only in his fifth year in Dawson, Tom O'Brien had already gained a reputation as hardworking and dependable, as had his brother, John, who ran the Phelps Dodge ranch in town, J. B. Dawson's old spread. Why, the year before, folks thought so well of Tom that he'd been asked to sign the state constitution, the document that helped bring New Mexico into statehood. O'Brien was a baseball fan, and as he worked that afternoon he may have been thinking of the World Series just completed, and how the Philadelphia Athletics had so easily trounced John McGraw's New York Giants.

Whatever was on O'Brien's mind, he was suddenly interrupted by a loud noise, a sharp report that people later compared to a high-powered rifle going off. Tom O'Brien looked at his pocket watch: it showed 3:10. The sound was followed by a muffled rumble, almost like a volcano erupting. It came, O'Brien immediately realized, from next door, from Mine Number Two, one of the oldest pits in Dawson, a mine that only a week before, O'Brien remembered, had been pronounced "in splendid condition" by the state mine inspector. Leaping to his feet, O'Brien raced across the room and hit a button that set off a siren heard by everybody in Dawson, it seemed, except the sleeping Hazel Henry.

Outside, O'Brien found flames reaching 100 feet from the mouth of Number Two, along with belching clouds of dense smoke. The stench of grease and burning oil filled the air. Soon, some of the 1,300 men from the other mines came running, their faces and clothes blackened, their carbide helmet lights still aglow. A small crowd followed them, shouting for information. From beneath a pile of rock and dirt near the mouth of Number Two, a miner clawed his way to the surface. He had been standing near the portal with a coworker, waiting for a tram car, when the explosion occurred, and rubble from the blast buried both men. The other man did not get up. In a few moments, three men, then three more, dazed and coughing, staggered out of the mine.

As the crowd grew, town supervisor T. L. Kinney arrived and stretched a rope across the front of the mine. With rocks packing the entrance to the mine, O'Brien donned a cumbersome oxygen mask and hurried over to Mine Number Five, where he knew a passageway led into Number Two. But more rocks plugged that tunnel as well as an air shaft that ran from the top of the mesa down into Number Two.

Back in his office, O'Brien put out the word for "helmet men," or rescue teams, and within the hour squads from Yankee and Tercio and Gardiner and Van Houten—all the St. Louis, Rocky Mountain and Pacific camps—were on their way to Dawson, as were striking miners from Ludlow, Colorado.

"I was only 200 feet away when the mine blowed up," says Mike Faba. "I was up there to give my brother-in-law some tobacco. I was only thirteen at the time, but I had already been working in the mines. Hell, you could work there when you were two years old then. I was a trapper boy first; you opened the doors so air could go in and out. Two miles in I worked. I had been laid off in August, 1913, so that's why I wasn't working that day. My father, Domenic, he hurt his thumb, so he didn't go in the mine that day either. When I got to the mine with the tobacco, a big black cloud of smoke come rolling out. I can still see it. Rocks flying, everybody running. My brother, Louie, he survived. Louie was close to the mouth of the mine. He felt his way in the dark. When he gets out, he keels over. Faints."

Even with the entries blocked and noxious gas surely caught inside, optimism prevailed, as far away as New York. "The mine is one of the model ones in the country," announced Cleveland H. Dodge, vice president of Phelps Dodge, when

Following the 1913 and 1923 explosions, crosses filled the town cemetery.

asked by the press about the explosion. In El Paso, a P.D. official said that there was nothing to suggest all the men would not be taken out of the mine alive. How many men? One figure said 300, though O'Brien eventually put the actual number at 284.

By Wednesday night, arc lights had been brought to the mine area, and as the weather turned chilly, the helmet men dug deeper. Behind T. L. Kinney's rope, the wait continued: men puffed cigarettes, women clutched rosaries, and toddlers wrapped themselves in blankets. The work went excruciatingly slow, and by 10:00 P.M. crews had only gone through the 100 feet of debris. Then, suddenly cheers went up as five men were brought out. Onlookers got another lift early Thursday when two more survivors were discovered. But joy turned to sorrow and tears when fourteen dead were found as well.

"I was only five years old," says Harmon Black, "but I remember my mother going next door to bake bread and roll bandages. Mrs. Bradford, the postmaster's wife, lived there. They rolled and baked and sent hot meals up for the boys getting the other ones out."

Standing near the portal of the mine, waiting for any news, was a young man who occasionally went to Tom O'Brien's office to use the only telephone at the site. When the boy spoke, it was always to his mother, the wife of William McDermott, general mine superintendent.

More help was on the way: the United States Bureau of Mines in Denver sent a rescue squad, and additional teams were ordered from Kansas and Wyoming. J. C. Roberts, Chief of the United States Mine Station in Denver, had been in Trinidad on business, and so he came down to take charge of the rescue efforts. A representative of the American Red Cross showed up with a check for $1,000, but Dawson officials, displaying the stubborn pride that would be the town's hallmark, turned down the money and said, "We can take care of ourselves."

A special train from El Paso pulled in Thursday morning, and with it came several surgeons and nurses, plus boxes of medical supplies, none of which would be of much use. By now, reporters had descended on Dawson. Newspaper correspondents from Raton, Albuquerque, Santa Fe, and Denver checked in, as well as writers from the Associated Press, *Collier's*, and *Harper's Illustrated Weekly*, and a photographer from *Pathé Weekly*. Dawson's reputation for safety intrigued many of the newsmen—"the impossible has happened," a P.D. official sighed twenty-four hours afterward—and few writers failed to mention in their stories that only a year before the *Titanic* had been called "unsinkable." The *New York Times* did not send a reporter, but its front-page headline a day later screamed "230 ENTOMBED IN MINE."

The hope that had hovered about Dawson dissipated by Thursday, due in part to the arrival of nine undertakers from towns around the state. The morticians were needed, since the corpses, often covered with tar paper, were starting to be brought out of Number Two in bunches. "As each body is recovered, it's placed on a wooden skid and drawn to the mouth of the mine by a mule," said the *Raton Range*. "Some bodies are burned almost to ash. Others are blown to pieces by the explosion."

Stories emerging from underground were indeed gruesome. Hands, arms, and heads poked from the rubble, said rescuers. One dead man was found leaning against a wall, his hands shielding a terror-stricken face. Another body was unearthed with pick in midair, as if trying to fight off the final landslide. Crews found an old miner reclining against a prop, with pipe in hand, as though he had fallen asleep. In truth, the man had died of deadly methane, the gas known as "fire damp."

"Everything that brawn and brain can do is being done," announced J. C. Roberts, chief of the rescue attempt. "This work is frightful. Many a time my brave assistants have sickened, and it was only by superhuman efforts that they have performed their task."

Fortunately, some inspiring stories made the rounds, too, such as the account of a giant Slav named Tomsik who had gone into the mine helmetless and rescued a young miner named Roy Simpleman.

A fire broke out in Number Two on Thursday afternoon, delaying rescue efforts for a time. That evening, one of the most tragic incidents of all occurred. James Laird and William Peyser, two helmet men from nearby Koehler, had rushed over to help as soon as they had heard of Dawson's disaster. Because the two volunteers were young and inexperienced, Roberts did not want them to go into the mine. But Laird and Peyser protested and went anyway. The pair, perhaps in an attempt to prove themselves, insisted on going deep into the mine, against the foreman's wishes. There, they worked at a furious pace, and, less than two hours later, their air ran out. Laird and Peyser tried to breathe from their oxygen cylinders, and when that failed, they panicked, threw down their apparatus, and ran. Poisonous gas killed them almost instantly.

The dead were taken to the old store downtown, where jet-black coffins, sent down from Denver, sat in stacks, like dominoes. Even with all the undertakers on hand, it wasn't easy to make identifications. The round check tags that miners carried were used when available, but often morticians had to go only by a piece of clothing. Many of the bodies were so badly mutilated that coffins simply bore the word *Unknown.*

"The death list in the Stag Cañon disaster is appalling," proclaimed the *Albuquerque Morning Journal.* Some distinguished visitors came to Dawson on Friday—J. S. Douglas, Jr., son of the president of Phelps Dodge and representatives from the Italian, Austrian, and Hungarian consulates in Denver. All had come to meet with families and offer assistance, though they must have quickly seen the bleakness of the task. "As you look from face to face upon the silent groups in the street," noted the *Raton Range,* "you see written one word: incomprehension."

By now, everyone knew the worst had happened. Slightly more than twenty survivors had been found, and expectations of finding more were small. Rescuers still had to timber as they went, and in some cases rocks 150 feet high stood in their paths.

On Friday afternoon there was a glimmer of hope when José Fernández, buried and unconscious, was brought out. But he turned out to be the last man to be found alive. Suddenly, Tom O'Brien, who had worked almost nonstop since Wednesday afternoon, dropped in exhaustion. As O'Brien was carried off, the crowd around him stood haggard, their eyes red-rimmed. "Everybody was crying," remembers Mike Faba, "and I cried with them. Then I went and told my sister, who was pregnant, that Luigi, her husband, was killed. He was only twenty-two, and they'd just gotten married. They'd gone to Raton in a horse and buggy for the wedding. I told her, 'Luigi, he got it.' They stayed up all night waiting for him, but he don't come home."

The world now knew of Dawson and its plight: cables begging for any scrap of news of kin arrived from nearly every corner of the globe. The fourth worst mining disaster ever, experts were calling it, though later it would rank second. While town officials worked to gain information for faraway

The Denver Post *sent a photographer
to record the aftermath of the 1913 disaster.*

relatives, T. L. Kinney, the law in Dawson, discovered he had another problem. Kinney had heard that a few members of the United Mine Workers of America, then just a fledgling union, had slipped into the community on the pretense of helping families hit by the disaster. To Kinney, a good company man, the UMWAers were troublemakers, and he ordered special security guards to run anyone suspicious out of town.

Big tragedies have a peculiar way of revealing little miracles. George Mavroidis had been working in Thirteen East of Number Two that Wednesday afternoon when a sudden rush of air doused his light. Then the gas had come, and sixteen men around Mavroidis had dropped like leaves. On his hands and knees, Mavroidis checked each man: not one was breathing. Then suddenly he blacked out. Mavroidis came to the next morning—in the mine office. Virginio Forni also was working in Thirteen East at the time of the explosion. But instead of rushing to the main entry with most of the others and being consumed by gas, Forni remained in his room and was taken out unconscious eighteen hours later. Resuscitated, he too, lived. A miner, who had left work early because his wife had asked him to get some scrip from the company store, missed dying by two minutes. Likewise, a motorman, who had derailed an outbound trip, went to summon help—only a minute before the blast. There was one more miracle: twenty-two mules had gone to work that day in Number Two. All the mules died—except a white one. He was found battered and blackened, ambling in a back chamber among a heap of dead men.

Rescue workers reached Eighteen East, on the "highline" side of the mine, on Saturday night. If crews had been pessimistic before, they abandoned all hope then, for here the body tally was astonishing. Among the many dead in this section was William McDermott, the general mine superinten-dent. McDermott's death was greatly mourned. The father of six children, he had started at the bottom of the coal business, as a miner in Colorado. McDermott did not have to be un-derground that day but had gone in only to check on a coal dust problem. "He was a very able and experienced man and highly esteemed for his personal worth," eulogized the *Raton Range*. Workers also found the body of Henry J. McShane, the idealistic nineteen-year-old son of a wealthy New York City couple who were principal stockholders in Phelps Dodge, lying near McDermott. McShane had gone to Dawson to ob-serve the family investment firsthand and to avoid being classified as one of the "idle rich." Many miners did not know McShane's background.

But everybody knew Alexander MacDonald, whose body also was unearthed. Originally from Trinidad, MacDonald had been a coal miner for fifty-two years. In Dawson and anywhere else he worked, MacDonald loved to stand in bars and recite the works of Robert Burns.

Almost all the coffins with identifiable remains went to individual graves in the local cemetery, just south of town, which at the time was a rather small plot. The dead who could not be positively identified were placed in an open trench there, an act that made good-byes difficult, for some mourners simply were not sure who was buried where. A few families did not even know a loved one had died. Because Mauro Martínez had left Mexico illegally to work in Dawson, he didn't tell Phelps Dodge of his next of kin. It would be some time before Martínez's family discovered his whereabouts.

Rev. Antonio Cellier from Springer said the Catholic Mass, and Rev. Harvey Shields, an Episcopal, and Rev. Sam Magill, a Presbyterian, came down from Raton to bury the Protestants.

Services were "mercifully brief," said the *Raton Range*. Phelps Dodge paid all funeral expenses—at a cost of $600 per day—and donated white iron crosses to mark the graves. Later, families added headstones or carved words in the markers in many languages but which almost always translated the same: "Rest in peace."

The turmoil surrounding the disaster made preparing bodies for shipment almost impossible. Some requests were granted, however. William McDermott was interred in Trinidad. Thomas Pattison was buried in Punxsutawney, Penn-sylvania. Henry McShane was buried in Dawson, only to be disinterred later, placed in a special vault, and sent to New York City, where a memorial service was held.

Twenty-three men survived the explosion. Fourteen got out on their own, and nine were rescued the night of the blast, all near the bottom of the air shaft. The final death count totaled 263. The vast majority of the dead were Italians—at least 130—and many of those were single men. Next came Greeks, then Mexicans, followed by a scattering of Slavs, Hungarians, and Poles, plus a Frenchman and a Russian. The English-speaking fatalities included a Scotsman, an Irishman (McDermott), and numerous Americans, including nine blacks.

By mid-November, all the bodies had been recovered and buried, and by early 1914 Number Two had reopened. P.D. estimated the shutdown had cut the company's coal output by one-quarter. In terms of property damage, the mine disaster was the worst on record.

Phelps Dodge did not look at the tragedy in terms of lost earnings. The company immediately gave each widow $1,000, more if the woman wanted to go back to Europe to relocate. Each child of a dead miner was given $200. The nearest relative of each single man was given $500. The compensation was considered extraordinarily generous for the time, and it was a service that P.D. continued in Dawson for as long as men there died in underground accidents.

All during the October vigil one man had stood in front of Number Two and said little. Rees H. Beddow, the state mine inspector, heard much, however. A lot of what Beddow heard had to do with the cause of the explosion. Nearly everyone blamed methane, CH_4, the odorless, colorless, tasteless but highly flammable gas.

Methane definitely was a risk factor in coal mining. The year before, Leopold Sluga, a mine worker in Dawson, had quit Stag Cañon in a huff because he felt there was too much fire damp there and that the mines would eventually blow. Coincidentally, Sluga returned to Dawson in 1913 to help out with the rescue effort.

Dawson's mines certainly had good safety reports, but that did not mean they would remain safe. In the previous year, five men had died in five different fatalities in Dawson. As early as 1903, there had been a major mine accident in Dawson, the community's first. On September 14 of that year, a curtain in Number One accidentally ignited, and flames fed by coal dust raced through the tunnels. Nearly 500 miners escaped. Three men trapped in the mine were a few feet from safety when another savage explosion ripped the pit and caused rescue workers to retreat, not before several had been seriously burned. The three trapped miners died. Was the mine safe? Only a short time before the explosion an inspector had said of it, "No dust, no gas; mine well timbered."

Beddow, no-nonsense administrator from Gallup, a hard-liner, did not like what people were saying about methane. The state mine inspector had spent much of October 15 and 16, a week before the explosion, inside Number Two. He had given the pit high marks for safety. Though he had found no standing gas, Beddow took a sample of main return air and sent it for analysis to the United States Bureau of Mines in Pittsburgh, Pennsylvania. The sample returned to Beddow showed .0019 percent methane, extremely low.

Gas did not cause the Dawson explosion, and Beddow knew it. William McDermott's interest in a coal dust problem confirmed that for him. Coal dust had only recently been determined to be a risk in mines, especially in New Mexico, where the great aridity increased the possibility of combustion, particularly when a ruptured ventilating system couldn't pull any of the dust out.

When Beddow first mentioned his coal dust theory, he found little support in Dawson. But two days after the explosion, Jo E. Sheridan, the former Territorial mine inspector and a highly respected geologist who knew the Stag Cañon operation well, told an Albuquerque newspaper, "It is not probable there was any great accumulation of gas at any point in the Dawson mines as these mines are among the best equipped for ventilation and safety appliances in the world."

If Beddow felt redeemed, there is no record of it. Instead of gloating, he began a careful examination of Number Two. On November 4 he released a report that said the explosion was triggered by coal dust. Though criticized for that presumptuous belief, Beddow stuck to his guns. On November 7, he released an even bigger bombshell: the explosion was caused by an overcharged shot. In other words, someone had placed an explosive in Number Two. Beddow even said where: Room Number Twenty-Seven, off the Ninth West Entry.

When the ensuing furor died down, Beddow explained that a miner, more than likely trying to increase his personal coal production, had badly loaded a few holes with dynamite. To secure the necessary voltage, the man had rigged a long copper wire to trolley line, instead of a firing line. The blast blew coal out into the mine and raised coal dust, which ignited immediately. The explosion spread through the mine as a flash fire, killing most of the men instantly. The guilty man had broken several company rules, the most serious being that he had set the charge when men were still in the mine.

If Dawsonites had trouble fathoming these findings, Jo Sheridan concurred with Beddow. "It is possible," Sheridan said, "that the powder men or a miner may have exploded some powder and thus started a dust explosion."

Beddow knew a miner was at fault; the powder men came into the mine after 7:00 P.M., when everyone was out of the pit. Only a month before, at Gallup's Heaton Mine, Beddow remembered, the same thing had happened. No one had been killed there, but three miners had been arrested.

No arrests would be made in Dawson, of course, for the miner who had loaded the charge had died along with 262 others. Nor did Beddow urge an investigation to name the man. In his annual report to New Mexico Governor William C. McDonald, Beddow did offer several recommendations, all of which Stag Cañon acted on. Shot firing would now be carefully supervised, and miners would no longer be allowed to load their own holes. Shot firers would go into a mine only when everyone else was out of it, and firing would be done electrically, from the outside, as it was supposed to have been done. Also, fire bosses would be on hand to double-check all the conditions of each face being worked on and to record those conditions in a notebook. Tightly sealed pit cars were introduced, and the size of mines was reduced.

Reports and recommendations do not necessarily encourage healing. That takes time, as Dawsonites discovered. In boardinghouses around town, vacant seats at dining tables stayed empty into 1914, out of respect. Less obvious was the fact that people did not talk about the explosion. John Sekot's father had been killed in Number Two, but Sekot never heard his mother speak of it. Nor did Avery Black, foreman of the tipple that afternoon in October, or Barney McGarvey, another tippleman, ever tell their children what they saw.

What Dawsonites did do was go back to work. Tom O'Brien returned to his desk at the mine office, where he labored faithfully as the Stag Cañon general manager for seven more years. O'Brien's niece, Hazel Henry, eventually took a job teaching school up at Loreta. And Judge T. L. Kinney went back to work at the Opera House, where, coincidentally his secretary was Tom Henry, Hazel's husband.

May Dee Lunsford stood among her third grade pupils at Central School in downtown Dawson and tried to show them how to make a mailbox for Valentine's Day, a week away. The big clock on the wall indicated almost 2:30 P.M. when suddenly a tremendous *ka-boom* shook the windows of the classroom like bedsheets.

"Mine explosion!" some of the children yelled simultaneously.

"Oh, no," said their teacher, a tall woman who not long before had come to Dawson from Texas. "That's probably just some blasting for the new houses." In fact, that week fifty coke breeze houses *were* being build all over town.

But the children, most of whom had been around Dawson longer than May Dee, insisted that what they had heard was a mine erupting.

Finally, the teacher went out into the hall where she spot-

THE DAWSON NEWS

Published Weekly by THE WELFARE DEPARTMENT

VOLUME III.   DAWSON, NEW MEXICO—   THURSDAY, FEBRUARY 15, 1923.   NUMBER 3.

Explosion in No. 1 Mine

One Hundred and Twenty-two Men Are Entombed. Two Come Out Alive. All but 14 Bodies Recovered

A terrific explosion occurred in No. 1 mine at 2.30 o'clock Thursday afternoon which has probably taken a toll of 120 lives, as it is not thought possible that any of the few remaining men in the mine will be brought out alive.

Immediately following the explosion, which was felt in nearly every section of Dawson, hundreds of people rushed to the vicinity of No. 1 mine, where a view of the demolished reinforced concrete portal of the mine confirmed their suspicion that the worst had happened.

Owing to precautions taken in connection with the installation of the mine fan, this equipment was not injured, and ventilation was quickly restored. Rescue crews were immediately organized, and within a few minutes after the explosion, W. D. Brennan, manager of the mines, led the first crew into the main entry. The preliminary exploration work revealed the fact that the overcasts and stoppings had been blown out and that the entry was almost impassable on account of the heavy caves and debris encountered. With the hundreds of trained rescue workers among the Dawson miners and the valuable assistance given by neighboring coal companies, the penetration of the mine in the hope of rescuing the unfortunate victims advanced as rapidly as the conditions would permit.

In the meantime a first aid station was established at the mine check cabin where the hospital staff of physicians and nurses ably assisted by a number of volunteer workers, were on duty to administer to those who might be injured or overcome with gas. At houses near by, preparations were also made to prepare food for those engaged in the rescue work. Before the first shift of rescue workers had returned from the mine, headquarters had been established for this relief work under the leadership of Mrs. Hanson of the Red Cross. Ably assisted by a number of the ladies of the camp, hot coffee and sandwiches were served as the different shifts came off duty.

As the night wore on, those gathered around the portal of the mine gradually went to their homes, but the grim work of the rescue men went on. Rescue crews of fifty men each under competent leadership continued their search for the dead bodies and brought them out as fast as they were located. In many places the falls of rock completely blocked the entry,

thus delaying the progress of the work. By morning, only six bodies had been recovered.

At 9.30 o'clock Friday morning, two of the entombed men, Charles Cantalie and Filini Martini, walked out of the mine unassisted. Hope was raised in the hearts of all that more men might be rescued, but there were no duplications of their miraculous escape. Uninjured by the terrific force of the explosion, and fully conscious of the deadly effect of the gas which follows in its wake, the two men demonstrated rare judgment in their effort for self-preservation. Stripping off some of their garments, they moistened them in water and held them over their faces to keep out the deadly gas. They then extinguished their lights, realizing that they would need them at such time as they might think that it was safe to endeavor to make their way to the outside. For over nineteen hours they waited; and then cautiously making their way over the debris which filled the entry, they walked out in safety. Seemingly they are none the worse for their experience.

According to the mine office records 140 men checked into the mine on the morning of Thursday, the 8th. Of this number, 18 left during the day, leaving 122 employed at the time of the explosion. It is evident that only two of this number have survived.

Within a few hours after the explosion occurred, offers of assistance began to pour into Dawson from surrounding coal camps and other points more distant. Rescue crews and equipment furnished by the St. Louis, Rocky Mountain and Pacific company, arrived early Thursday morning. By 2.30 o'clock the following morning, two mine rescue cars of the Colorado Fuel and Iron Company, in charge of George Parker, had also arrived. Word was later received that Bureau of Mines Cars No. 1 and 2 had been ordered to Dawson. These cars arrived Saturday afternoon and their attendant crews immediately joined in the rescue work which was already under way.

Throughout the several days which have passed since this catastrophe, the operation of the several departments that must necessarily function in a crisis of this kind have established a more or less definite routine. The work of the welfare department and that of the Red Cross has been coordinated and the relief work in the homes handled in a systematic man-

ner. Provisions and other articles of necessity were delivered to those in need and effort made to console the bereft. The teachers of the Dawson schools were of valuable assistance in all of this relief work.

As the bodies were recovered from the mine, they were taken to a morgue established at the rescue station and prepared for burial. They were then taken to the opera house, where anxious relatives and friends awaited, or to the homes from which private funerals were held.

Friday night a coroner's jury, consisting of Celso Chavez, Ralph Trini, Jake Grubecek, J. Q. Welch, Frank Moorehead and Paul K. Carson was sworn in by Judge Kinney. The members of the jury have viewed the bodies as they have been brought from the mine, but as yet have made no investigation as to the cause of the explosion.

It is estimated that it will require at least two months to put the mine in shape for operation.

Men who came out alive: Charles Cantalie, Filini Martini.

Bodies recovered: Nick Arvas, Martin Kemp, Paul Stamos, Frank Tomasoni, Gust Scopelitis, Ernesto Tozzi, Frank Rounika, Alessandro Zanoni, George W. Leeming, Criss Scopelitis, Anton Lira, Tomasi Guiseppe, Antonio Geromino, Francisco Romero, Evagelos P. Chiboukis, Nick J. Retsias, Antonio Scantalia, Angelo Palumbo, Claud Litchford, Marcial Alamillo, Nick Volanis, Jesus Barranco, Anacledo Alamillo, Mike Stavovich, Odorino Gatti, Frank Nardini, Floryan Papis, George Liguzos, Geo. K. Payhas, Josef Pokorn, Earl Graves, Ben H. Mullins, John Janakas, Tony Zanoni, Georgis Kallas, Harry Morrison, Joe Cortez, Burley Cenotto, Earl Duke, Albert E. English, Alec Kerr, Clifton C. Estes, W. R. Holmes, Rode Maricich, Fred Trujillo, Albert English, Roy Trujillo, Antonio Montoya, Pete Santilla, Joe Delost, Mike Kapich, Luigi Cassai, Jim Lorenzo, Pacifico Santi, Pete Vucinish, Nick Papas, George Markis, John Dallas, John Karamougis, Nick Perovich, Elia Vulanovich, Mike Gayovich, John Stoynoff, Gennera Gatti, Alex Aguilar, Julian Dominguez, Fermin Gallegos, Panfilo Cordova, Filiberto Valpando, Juan Pinedo, Julian Archuletta, Felix Gardea, Cruz Rodriguez, Gios Marachino, Nazzarene Curzi, Baldo Pellegrini, Frenche Bonaventura, Carlo Necas, Isadora Gomez, Ben Sena, Miguel Rosales, Juan Cruz, Jose Anastacio Maestas, Gregario Duran, William S. Davies, Gabino Calderian, Manuel R. Ybarra, Manuel Ybarra, Secundio Ybarra, Weneslado Masiaz, J. Austin Green, E. C. Fimpel, Jesus Mares, John Wilson, Al Trujillo, Matt Gasparac, J. A. Mondragon, Alonzo Cartazar, Christ P. Costa, George Charette, Louis Capen, Tony Oblock, Leandro Gonzales. Of the seventeen names below, three have been taken from the mine but have not been identified, the

LOYALTY OF DAWSON PEOPLE COMMENDED BY W. D. BRENNAN

I desire at this time to express, on behalf of the company and myself, a deep appreciation of the loyalty and assistance rendered by the employes and officials of the Stag Canon Branch of Phelps Dodge Corporation during this great calamity which has fallen upon us all.

I wish especially to thank those who first entered the mine after the fateful accident, and those who subsequently carried on the exploration and rescue work at great risk of their lives, and to whom the entire community is grateful for their untiring efforts in recovering its dead.

Without the assistance of the women who so freely rendered their assistance in preparing and serving food and refreshments to the workmen, the work would have been greatly delayed and handicapped.

W. D. BRENNAN, Manager,
PHELPS DODGE CORP.,
Stag Canon Branch.

SCOT DUPONT INJURED

Scot Dupont, underground superintendent, was just entering Number One mine at the time of the explosion and was blown back several feet and sustained burns and cuts about the face and was otherwise injured by the force of the explosion. He did not leave duty until he collapsed.

Among the others who were slightly injured were Andie Seppie, Elmer Sherfick and Gabe Zellers. All three were in the motor barn at the time.

AN APPRECIATION

I desire to express to the members of the Knights of Pythias and Masons, to the doctors and nurses at the hospital, and to many friends, my sincere appreciation of their attention during my confinement in the hospital.

ERNEST L. INGLEDUE.

FATHER AND SON BANQUET POSTPONED

The Father and Son banquet being arranged by the Dawson Boy Scouts at the lodge room in the opera house Monday evening, was indefinitely postponed.

Announcement was also made that there would be no troop meeting during the coming week.

Mr. George Vigil left Monday for Los Angeles. He was accompanied as far as aton by Mr. and Mrs. F. A. Vigil, daughter Virginia, and a number of friends.

other fourteen being the ones still to be recovered at noon today:

Pete Kapich, Aaron Simpson, Higinio Herrera, Ben Marlar, Cruz Gomez, Santiago Gomez, Felix de Abila, Manuel de la Luz, Anton Kobana, Martin Torres, Audrey Gonzales, William H. Lawson, Thomas McNeish, James Howard, Luigi Bressili, Marselino Velasquez, Pat Chavez.

Not surprisingly, the town newspaper gave front-page coverage to the 1923 explosion.

ted her principal, Susie Young. "Is it true?" May Dee asked.

Young nodded. "In Number One."

The date was Thursday, February 8, 1923. In Washington, D.C., President Warren Harding was steering a leaky ship; in New York City, heavyweight boxing champion Jack Dempsey couldn't figure out who to fight next; and in cold, blustery Dawson, a town that had grown to 4,200 people, a terrible accident had happened once again.

Two miles up the canyon, Scott Dupont, who now had the job William McDermott had held ten years before, had gone into Number One, the first mine opened in Dawson, just minutes before. When an outgoing trip of cars approached Dupont only a short distance in, the general superintendent stepped back. Just as he did a blast nearly burst his eardrums and sent him sprawling to the ground. Though he suffered a concussion, singed hair, and a cut face, Dupont struggled to his knees and crawled out of the mine. William D. Brennan, who had taken over for Tom O'Brien, as general manager, sounded the siren this time. Brennan, a steadfast P.D. executive, knew instantly the blast had hit Number One. His records showed that 140 men had checked in that morning, but that 18 had left during the day, mostly because of illness. That meant 122 men, more than a tenth of the town's work force, were still in the pit. Only a few days before, Brennan recalled, the state mine inspector had made a thorough tour of all ten of Dawson's mines. He had pronounced Number One, in words that had a familiar ring, "in excellent condition." Dust in the mines, the man had said, was being contained very well.

But there was no time to think about that now; help was needed urgently. One of Brennan's first tasks was to send a telegram to that inspector. At 3:20 P.M., Worthington W. Risdon, New Mexico's state mine inspector, a man known for his meticulousness, received this terse message at his Albuquerque office: "Number One mine exploded at two-thirty. No details. W. D. Brennan."

Risdon hurried to his home on Roma Street and told his wife, Ophelia, that he had to leave town. Then, like his counterpart Rees Beddow a decade before had done, he immediately got on the next train to Dawson.

Once again a crowd began to gather at the front of a Dawson mine—women and children mostly, all wearing fearful expressions. And once again the venerable Judge T. L. Kinney pulled a rope across the front of a mine's portal. Kinney was getting used to calamities: besides playing a role during the 1913 disaster, he had managed the community's quarantine efforts during the big influenza epidemic of 1918.

The force of this blast, if not greater than the one in 1913, surely was as powerful. A monstrous crater sat in the side of the mountain where Number One once opened. The explosion had sent huge chunks of the reinforced concrete portal, some pieces weighing half a ton, out across the canyon—"Like paper being blown to atoms," said the *Raton Range.* Flying debris demolished a metal car barn and injured three men inside.

Naomi McCarty was in her backyard getting water when the blast occurred, and the force of it made her drop her dipper. Sabina DiLorenzo was baby-sitting her infant brother, Toby. "All of a sudden I heard a big sound: I thought it was thunder." A fifth grade student at Central School, Vernice Smock was sent home when the explosion rocked the town. "I was threatened with dire death by my father and mother if I went up there," she says. Celso Chávez did go up to the mine. "I was in manual training class at the Downtown School when we heard the blast. Mr. Dye was our teacher. Several of

Four days after Mine Number One blew up in 1923 rubble still covered the mine entrance.

the boys in the class, Henry Dupont, Terence Scanlon, they had fathers up at the mine, so there was worry. Right away we jumped into Mr. Dye's car. There were about five or six of us kids in that car. When we got to the entrance of the mine, there were people moaning and all. But Mr. Dupont was out there directing traffic. He had just been inside the mine a short time before. Mr. Scanlon, he was in the electrician's office, so he was okay, too."

Harmon Black, by now a strapping young man of almost sixteen, was in geometry class up at the high school on Capitan Hill. "The blast broke windows in the school. The whole place dumped out. Damn right you could hear it. We knew exactly what happened." For a second time Black's mother made food for rescue workers, only now at the Mercantile, where the company provided roast beef sandwiches and coffee. Up at the explosion site, Elizabeth Hanson directed a cadre of Red Cross-trained relief workers. Nearby, May Dee Lunsford had volunteered to hand out food, but she found the job difficult. Whenever she passed a sandwich to a worker, May Dee turned her head away: the gas fumes on the men's clothes were so strong she nearly gagged.

Rescuers had it easier than in 1913. The ventilation system had not been damaged, so crews would not have to enter the mine wearing bulky oxygen masks. Two bodies were found just inside Number One, and, as crews worked, it quickly became apparent that nearly everyone had been killed—instantly. Newspaper and wire service reporters once more poked around for stories, many of which used the phrase "death revisits Dawson." Even the *New York Times* headline the following day nearly duplicated the one used in 1913: "EXPLOSION ENTOMBS 122 MINE WORKERS."

Indeed, the similarities between the two disasters were

striking. As in 1913, the 1923 explosion yielded numerous heartbreaking stories, and one of the saddest concerned the English family. Albert English had gone to work that day in Number One, accompanied by his son, Albert, Jr., a foreman who was filling in for an ailing coworker. When rescue teams formed, Fred English, Albert, Jr.'s younger brother, was one of the first to sign on. If Fred took heavy steps that day, he had a reason. Ten years before another brother, Arthur English, had died in the explosion of Number Two. This newest disaster so upset Fred's mother that just the sound of it sent her screaming into her yard.

However, there were miracles this time as well, just as there had been in 1913. Scott Dupont's step backward just before the explosion had surely saved his life. Jay Cericola, bound for Number One, had forgotten his lunch bucket that morning, but when he got home to fetch it, he decided not to go back to work. Federico Rivera, also slated to work Number One, had been up all night drinking and gambling in a bar at Loreta. He finally lurched home at 3:00 A.M. When Rivera got up that morning, his wife told him to go back to bed. "You might get fired if you go to work," she said.

At 5:30 A.M. Friday, as W. W. Risdon stepped off a train in Dawson, he detected an uncharacteristic grimness that had taken over the town. Already a squad of undertakers had arrived, and coffins were on the way from every available source. Still, rescue workers, including the recovered Scott Dupont, units from Tucson and Hanna, Wyoming, and fresh teams from the United States Bureau of Mines in Denver and the Colorado Fuel and Iron Company, refused to give up hope. Their confidence received an enormous boost later that morning when two miners, the first survivors of the explosion, walked out of Number One unaided. Charles Skandale, from

Crete, and Felini Martini, an Italian, had been inside for almost twenty hours, and when they appeared shouts of joy rose from the crowd. "You're the only ones to live!" sobbed Skandale's wife, Elizabeth. After the two miners had been resuscitated and had been given something to drink and eat, they told an amazing story.

Assigned to the deepest part of the pit, to an area called Crosscut Number Four North, the pair had been thrown to the ground in the blast, like everyone else. Both men knew enough to tear off their wool sweaters, dip the material in Martini's water pail, which somehow hadn't turned over, and then put the sweaters over their mouths and noses to filter out the deadly gases. Fearful that calling out would cause them to inhale toxic air, the two lay there in silence. Though Skandale and Martini heard voices in another room, they didn't move. "I prayed and thought of my boys, Nick and George, and my wife," Skandale told reporters. "Then suddenly I felt a breath of fresh air in my face. I touched Felini, and we took off our bandages. *The air was sweet!* We knew they were pumping it in and we were saved."

Hours went by, and the voices eventually ceased. Finally, Skandale and Martini decided to get up and try to find a way out. Years later people claimed the two were led to safety by holding the tail of a mule that walked them out. But instead the miners had stumbled out on their own, first over four men they had heard talking hours before, but who were now dead. Their helmet lights not working, they tripped over debris and boulders, and felt their way past ripped timbers and mangled machinery. They were still staggering, still holding sweaters over their mouths when rescuers found them.

The day after the rescue, a United Press reporter interviewed Skandale at his Dawson home. "You're not going back into

Charles Skandale (fourth from the left in the front row) at the burial for 1923 victims. Skandale was one of only two survivors of that mine disaster.

the mine anymore, are you?'' the reporter asked, aware that the miner's younger brother, Tony, died in the explosion. Skandale, holding his two sons close, looked puzzled. ''Why sure,'' he said. ''I'm a miner.''

As the search for more men went on, telegraph operators worked sixteen-hour shifts in the depot. One of the first messages came from the Italian ambassador: ''Italy follows with motherly love every step of her sons gone abroad to give their work and often lives in fostering the progress and prosperity of humanity.'' Most of the wires were, as before, from overseas. Helping to staff the makeshift communications center was Harvey Springer, Dawson's postmaster. Springer had an empathy for the goings-on: he had once been a miner.

Chief telegram delivery boy was Harmon Black, hired because of his *Denver Post* paper route in the town. Says Black: ''We'd get a telegram for, say, Joe Brozovich, and it would go, 'Joe, are you dead?' I knew the Brozoviches lived in second row over in Seven Camp, so I delivered the message to the family and got a tip. In four days I made $138 delivering telegrams. I made more than my father made in a month.''

On Friday evening, T. L. Kinney swore in a coroner's jury consisting of six prominent Dawsonites. The panel's job was to inspect the bodies and, if possible, determine causes for the explosion. Those bodies had been taken first to a substation in the Community Church for embalming. Harmon Black, when he wasn't delivering telegrams, peeked into the church's sanctuary. ''The bodies were all stiff, with their arms up in the air, like they knew they were going to be buried by rock. The morticians were cutting clothes off 'em; sometimes the clothes were burned right into 'em.'' Identification once again was made by any means available. When a charred corpse was brought in with a lump of gold fused to its head, Giuseppe

Arcangeli was eventually summoned. Arcangeli, someone remembered, had a boarder at his house known for his gold teeth. Placed in rough pine caskets, the dead were taken to the Opera House, where they awaited burial on a stage that had most recently been occupied by a vaudeville troupe called the Mayme Arington Associate Players.

P. G. Beckett, general manager of Phelps Dodge Corporation in Douglas, Arizona, arrived on Saturday morning in a raging snowstorm to learn the death toll stood at seventy-five and climbing. The bad weather drove away many of the people standing vigil, but excavators plowed on. That evening, Fred English came upon the broken body of his father. Fred's brother, Albert, Jr., would be found later that night, also dead.

By Sunday, more than 4,000 sandwiches had been served to rescue workers, who now were beginning to wind down their efforts. Walter Goodhue and Leonard Wood, hired at $3 a day, had been digging graves for two days already. Goodhue also made extra money by watching the town cemetery at night, as ghoulish souvenir hunters had been reported. Outside the Opera House, caskets were placed aboard an old-fashioned, wagonlike hearse, pulled down Main Street to the cemetery by two white mules.

A small procession usually followed. Curiously, the mules needed only one trip before they had the procedure down. They would wait stock-still as a casket was lowered into the ground, and for either Father Joseph Couturier, Dawson's Catholic priest, or Sam Magill, the Protestant minister from Raton, to speak. As soon as the service concluded, the mules turned on their own and went back for another body. Since the nearest Russian Orthodox priest was in Pueblo, Colorado, and there was no time for him to make the trip down, burial services for the half-dozen Montenegrans and a Bulgarian were held in Raton.

Once more Phelps Dodge paid for everything, including another set of white iron crosses. Italians again dominated the fatality list, which finally numbered 120. Only Skandale and Martini survived.

The tragedy left more than 100 children fatherless, more than fifty women widows. Harry Morrison and Earl Graves, two dryland farmers from Cherryvale, New Mexico, east of Las Vegas, had been working as Dawson miners during the slack growing season. Both men were killed. Morrison left a widow and six children, Graves a widow and four children.

As it had done a decade earlier, Phelps Dodge compensated women and children handsomely and offered relocation, which in some instances meant a forced relocation if they couldn't find work. Unlike after the previous disaster, the company's 1923 reparations occasionally were challenged. Mabel Charette, sister of a mule driver named George Charette, who was killed in the 1923 explosion, sued the Stag Cañon Fuel Company. Mabel claimed she was dependent on George and the $30 a week he brought home. Before the explosion, miner Nick Perovich, who was single and childless, had sent a portion of his pay to his elderly parents in Europe. After Perovich died in the blast, his cousin petitioned P.D. to continue that financial aid.

Phelps Dodge showed its kindness in ways other than money. On the front page of the *Dawson News,* William Brennan, the branch manager, thanked townspeople for their loyalty ''during this great calamity which has fallen upon us all.'' P. G. Beckett added, ''The heroism and courage shown under very trying conditions by the families who have suffered a grievous loss has been a magnificent example to all.''

Those weren't merely corporate mouthings. ''I never saw a community close ranks as Dawson did in that explosion,'' says Harmon Black. ''There was no difference between bosses and workers; everybody was for the miners. There was no friction. It was simply a matter of getting in to those people and getting 'em out.''

Rescuers removed the body of the last fatality, Pete Kapich, from Number One on February 20. Later that year the mine resumed operations. With two major catastrophes now on its record, Stag Cañon for the first time had difficulty attracting new employees—at least regionally. When company recruiters hired Charles Cimino in 1924, they found him in northern California. To help deal with Dawson's somewhat tarnished reputation, only a year after the disaster in Number One Phelps Dodge printed a slick, twenty-page brochure that extolled life in the town. Not a word in the promotional piece mentioned the explosions. The *Dawson News* that same year spotlighted a story in which Daniel Harrington, supervising engineer of the United States Bureau of Mines in Denver, said, ''The Dawson mines are the most safely operated coal mines that I have ever come across.''

Was Dawson jinxed? Why did such bad things happen in such a good place? Coal mining has always been a dangerous occupation; Dawson just seemed to have more than its share of danger—call it bad luck—in the form of tragic accidents. And, as soon as the latest accident occurred, the word around town was a familiar one: gas. Methane, that evil fire damp, feared by miners everywhere, had to have caused this explosion.

Gas for a second time took all the blame until the coroner's jury released its report on February 14, 1923. The jury said the explosion resulted when a trip of thirty-five loaded coal cars went off the track. The derailment knocked down timbers to which a trolley feed line was attached. That in turn raised a

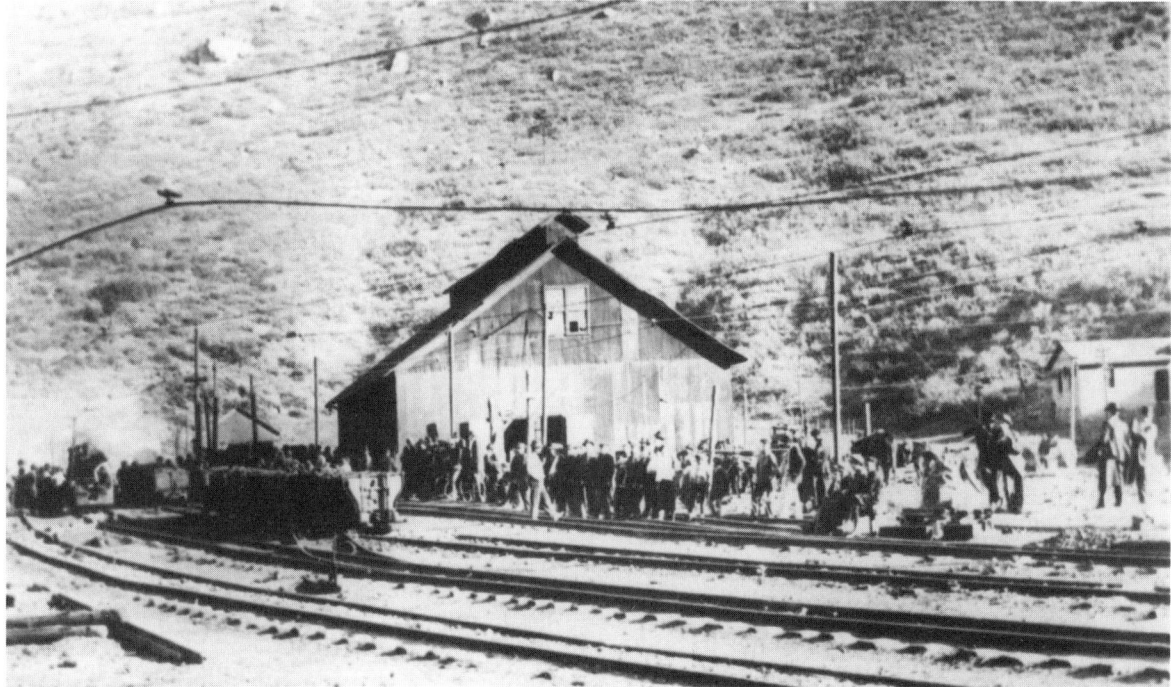

In 1923, Dawsonites waited for news in front of the Mine Number One, a scene that nearly duplicated 1913 events.

quantity of coal dust that was ignited by an electric arc, resulting from the feed wire coming in contact with one of the iron pit cars.

Coal dust once more became the culprit. As had been learned in 1913, bituminous coking coal of Dawson contained very flammable particles, but it had taken ten more years for people to understand those particles were far more threatening than gas.

The coroner's jury found that for almost five days there had been little or no water sprinkled in Number One. The huge fans, which fed the model ventilating system, drove so much air through the workings that any moisture quickly evaporated.

Worthington Risdon, the state mine inspector, had sensed all along that the problem was coal dust. In fact, during his examination Risdon found the site where the explosion originated, about 1,200 feet from the portal. Here, the jagged remains of the coal cars showed him that the force blasted outward to the entrance and back along the main tunnel.

Risdon accepted the coroner's report and then, reminiscent of Rees Beddow, added a startling postscript: "I have been told, by men in charge of the mine, that on February 3, five days before the explosion, someone closed a valve in the pipeline, thus shutting off the sprays and stopping the flow of water through the pipes. The extreme cold weather froze the water in the pipeline and therefore the mine had not had any water on the roads for five days preceding the explosion.'' As his predecessor had done in 1913, Risdon blamed the explosion on human error. And just as had happened in 1913, a feeling of disbelief, then acceptance, followed. No one in Dawson wanted to know who the careless man was, for what would be the point.

Risdon didn't just bear bad news; he brought recommendations to New Mexico Governor James F. Hinkle, and P.D. put them in place at Stag Cañon almost immediately. Ninety dust barriers were installed as a means of limiting the extent of an explosion. Six miles of waterlines were laid, with sprinklers and hoses extending to all working faces. Nine miles of mine roads were sprayed, or mudited, with fire-retardant adobe, as were roofs and ribs. In addition, P.D. studied the possibility of using storage batteries to operate locomotives, which would do away with power wires in the mines, contributing factors in both the 1913 and 1923 tragedies.

Some Dawsonites used the tragedy to remember. Each year on February 8, Charles Skandale, one of the two survivors, stayed home from work. On the one year he ventured out, for a shopping trip to Raton, Skandale was seriously injured in an automobile crash. For others, the disaster was something to forget. John McCarty, a member of a local rescue team, couldn't sleep at night for a long time afterward. Celso Chávez's father, Celso, Sr., had been a member of the coroner's jury, and the pain of that duty stopped him from ever once talking of it with his son. T. L. Kinney, who had now endured two horrors close-up, kept forever silent about both.

As they had done in 1913, most Dawsonites in the spring of 1923 simply found going back to work the best means of dealing with the past. Mike Faba stayed on in town to work the mines for another year and then left—for good. ''I went to Detroit, Michigan,'' he says. ''I wanted to see what was on the other side of the hill. And I didn't want to see no more people get killed.''

Chapter Six

LEARNING

*"If you went to school, you graduated;
if you went to church, you sat still."*
—Grayce Padilla Britton

Every weekday morning, at approximately 7:45, George Fenlon left his white-with-green-trim house near the base of Capitan, the most prominent hill in Dawson, and began walking up a well-worn footpath. Dressed in a gray worsted suit purchased at the Phelps Dodge Mercantile, and wearing a four-in-hand, high starched collar and blucher shoes with a glossy shine, his dark hair sharply parted on the side and spectacles framing his pleasant face, Fenlon was the model of tidiness. His routine also bespoke orderliness. In fact, by the time he reached the high school on the summit of Capitan and entered his second-floor office there, it was almost always 7:50.

After working all morning, shortly before noon Fenlon left his desk and headed back down the hill to home. There he ate lunch with his wife, Josephine—in warm weather Fenlon loved to dine on watermelon—and then climbed in his maroon Studebaker to retrieve the mail at the post office on Main Street, as well as stop by Central School. Those duties accomplished, he drove home and then again began the hike back up Capitan. By 5:00, when Fenlon had read the last piece of paperwork on his desk, he went once more down the hill. Dawsonites learned they could set their pocket watches by George Fenlon, for as the town's superintendent of schools he climbed and descended the hill behind his house at the same

Downtown's Central School, as all other schools in the community, played a key role.

times each day for almost twenty years.

Its mines, athletic teams, and multiethnic makeup gave Dawson distinction, but perhaps the town's greatest attribute was its schools. And efficient, systematic George Fenlon, a gentleman with a love for learning and some hard-to-break work habits, was responsible for the first-class quality of those classrooms.

Education in Dawson didn't start out as a model program. In 1902, the forty students in the newly organized camp were schooled beneath a makeshift tent. When the next year's attendance had climbed to 101, village officials knew it was time to build. The Downtown School, a wooden, two-story structure near the entrance to the community, went to seventh grade, but after that students were more or less on their own. The first high school, established in 1908, really wasn't a high school, for it stopped at the eighth grade. By 1914, two more grades had been added, and the enrollment had shot all the way to ten. Dawsonites paid $1 annually to finance the school, and presumably didn't grumble about it. Maude Freeman, the superintendent in those days, traveled to classes on horseback.

For several of those early years, most upper-level Dawson students went back and forth to Raton to pick up classes. The onset of World War I, and the productivity in the mines— Phelps Dodge enjoyed a 200 percent profit in Dawson in 1915—brought many more workers, and thus more children, to the town. By 1917, Dawson's population had grown to 2,000, and there were four schools, although there still was no senior high school, and one of the schools up the canyon at Loreta had only one teacher. Some sort of control was needed for the system to keep pace with the town's growth. The school board, as it would be for most of Dawson's existence, was composed of several ranking Phelps Dodge employees who wanted the best for their children. Recognizing the educational deficiency, P.D. sent out a call for an adept superintendent. Dawson found one in a proper, methodical, and dedicated math teacher from Nebraska named George Louis Fenlon.

Fenlon was only thirty-four when he came to Dawson, but he had already served as a school principal in Trinidad, Colorado, and at nearby Folsom, New Mexico, experience that earned him the title "Professor." If Professor Fenlon was shocked by the fact that Dawson High School that year had thirty-two students but only one teacher, and that some of the grade school teachers in town possessed only eighth-grade educations, he did not make an issue of it. Instead, Fenlon saw Dawson's potential, and went right to work to upgrade the town's school system.

One of the first things Fenlon did was require birth certificates for any child registering, the first school district in New Mexico to do so. Next, he set up night classes in English and American citizenship for adults. By 1924, sixty had graduated from the "Naturalization" course. He also insisted that teachers make home visits. With the board of education's blessing, Fenlon sought to construct the best buildings and to hire the finest teachers. Finally, Fenlon decreed that no young man could leave school and go in the mines unless he was sixteen and had received from Fenlon a lecture on life without knowledge. Prior to Fenlon's ruling, boys as young as twelve had been known to work in the mines.

Discipline—spanking, slapping, paddling—became a staple in the Dawson schools under Fenlon. So did name changes. "My second grade teacher, she couldn't pronounce my first name—*Massimino,*" says Mike Faba. " 'Your name's Mike,' she said, and so it stuck."

With more and more students entering Dawson classrooms and staying in them, school life gradually became the center of town life. An early Fenlon achievement was the completion of the new high school in 1921, which became an axis around which life in Dawson regularly revolved. There had been only one high school graduate in 1920, but with a brand-new stone building in 1921 there were eight. Named for James Douglas, the corporation president who died in 1918, the building was grand. With the Douglas grade school on the ground floor, and a high school that ran grades seven to twelve up above, with twelve classrooms and a library with 700 volumes, the building cost $100,000, a huge sum at the time. Mr. and Mrs. Cleveland E. Dodge traveled from New York City

Most single women teachers in Dawson lived in the Teacherage.

to dedicate the structure, for P.D. was as proud of it as Dawson.

Within a short time, thirty-three teachers were working in six different schools around Dawson. By 1922, there were 1,300 students, some even from neighboring coal camps, kids whose parents had heard glowing reports of the Dawson system. Things grew so fast that fourth grade teacher Ona Randall had seventy-five kids in her class in 1924. The high school experienced the biggest spurt, thanks in large part to Fenlon's encouragement. The superintendent helped students develop a yearbook, *Ye Coke Breeze,* that ran an impressive eighty pages in its first year; and he pushed for the formation of a dramatic club and a debating team. He also helped start a domestic science department (hat-making, anyone?) and had Victrolas placed in every classroom in town. Once Fenlon saw how interested Dawsonites were in athletics, and how sports could unify the town, he helped the high school organize its first basketball and football teams and was always on the lookout for the best coaches available.

As Dawson progressed, education prepared young people for life outside a coal mining town.

Fenlon also was instrumental in getting the Teacherage established in 1921. Here, single women—the only females allowed to run a classroom in Dawson—could find room and board for as little as $5 per month, in a modern, steam-heated, three-level Victorian-looking building.

Good teachers, Fenlon knew, were at the core of a good education, and he went after the elite. It wasn't always easy to attract the best ones, however, for on first glance Dawson, with its belching smokestacks and cindery slag piles, was not an overwhelmingly appealing community. Lulamay Brannon accompanied her husband, Leroy, to town in the summer of 1938. The Brannons had been living in Rifle, Colorado, where Leroy taught science and coached. "We drove in, and there were tracks and coal cars and dry dust blowing," says Lulamay. "Isolated way back up in that canyon—well, it looked awful." Fenlon wanted Brannon badly, and so was finally able to convince the couple to stay. "When we moved in," says Lulamay, "we saw things looked different. Dawson looked beautiful—not dusty or dark, but pretty! There were roses growing everywhere."

Dawson teachers were well known for their willingness to help a pupil reach his potential. Thus, most Dawson students developed a favorite teacher. For Lucille Hubbard Shipe, it was Grace Campbell, who taught high school English and who inspired her classes to learn things not merely for the sake of learning. For Marcia McClary Beall, it was Greg Randall, a music teacher who didn't mind asking the school band to practice outside until after dark and who made his students actually learn to like it. For Arthur Lucero, it was Margaret Mueller, a grade school teacher who saw nothing odd about teaching Lucero, crippled since birth with cerebral palsy, to read and write when he was twelve. For Tillie Zauhar Christie, it was Emogene Chase, who constantly urged her students to attend business schools out of state, although many of them had never traveled outside Dawson.

Some teachers in Dawson were institutions. Alice Devlin taught primary school and was the longtime principal of Douglas School. A small, thin woman who loved to wear big pink hats, Devlin was a tough taskmaster, an eccentric, and perhaps the first woman to climb Mount Baldy, near Eagle Nest. Never married, and bilingual, Devlin was trained in first aid and rescue work from almost the moment she came to Dawson to teach in 1915. She was still teaching there in 1950 when the town closed. Devlin took particular interest in children who didn't speak much English, working with them after school and during recess, admonishing them over and over: "Make something of yourself! Learn! Learn!"

Josephine Marcelli Andazola recalls that "Miss Devlin used to go to homes and visit with parents and tell them how their children were doing. How many teachers would do that today? She would come to our house, and my uncle, Guido Nizzi, who knew English, would be there to interpret."

Another memorable teacher was Hannah McGarvey, known to all as "The Whippin' Teacher." A sixth grade instructor and later principal of Central School, McGarvey seldom spared the rod—in her case, a piece of rubber hose. A peppy Irish woman who frowned more than she smiled, McGarvey nonetheless cared enormously for Dawson. Like Devlin, McGarvey taught in the town for four decades, and still would have been there at the end if a school had been open.

As Don Wilson remarks, "When Hannah McGarvey was teaching, she really showed what a giving person she was. I remember we had a boy named Raymundo Lopez, whose dad worked on the ranch. Raymundo was unlearnable; probably today you'd say he was dyslexic. But Hannah sat down next to him in the very back seat and special taught him in every subject. *Read it again! Read it again!'* I can still hear her saying. Raymundo stayed in Hannah's sixth grade class for at least a couple of years, probably more. But I bet he learned to read."

Before Herbert Bailey came to Dawson in 1931, music there had a patchy past. Arriving for an inspection tour of the town in 1913, Dr. James Douglas, president of Phelps Dodge Corporation, had been met at the depot by baker Louis Savio's municipal band, a ragtag bunch of mostly Italian miners. Douglas enjoyed the concert, but felt the musicians would sound better if properly attired. Thus, he had the Stag Cañon Branch manager order fifty spiffy uniforms and had the bill

Prestige and admiration followed Dawson's high school bands wherever they went.

sent to P.D. Savio later organized a school band, but he had no academic training. Bailey, a likeable, erect, college-trained Kansan who played the cornet, changed all that. During his twelve years in the town, Bailey, in the tradition of Harold Hill of *The Music Man* fame, made music a significant force in Dawson, teaching scores of students, including Greg Randall, his successor, to play musical instruments during study hall and after school. Bailey formed vocal groups and had his high school musicians give band concerts in the Opera House. He also organized the Northeastern New Mexico Music Festival, held during the first week of May each year in Raton, and helped drive the Dawson band to football and basketball games, leading them on as they marched about in red and black capes, and smiling as they turned heads and won every award in sight.

Fenlon didn't merely hire teachers; he also fired them. In the early days, he let women go who even casually mentioned they might be getting married. Fenlon didn't allow female teachers to smoke in public, and he would not put up with any fooling around from male teachers. A teetotaler, Fenlon was not amused if he heard that one of the men on his staff had been seen stepping into the Snake.

As fine a staff as Fenlon brought to Dawson, no member of it was ever greatly compensated. Indeed, when Alice Devlin was teaching, she had to buy her own colored paper and phonics charts as well as control as many as 120 students at once, many who didn't speak English. All this for $675 a year. Early on, Phelps Dodge had helped the school system cover budget deficits. But, when the town began to decline in numbers, that no longer happened. Dawson did its best to hold on to its good teachers, though that wasn't always possible. In 1943, music teacher Herbert Bailey was slated to earn $2,400 a year from a $44,479 budget. When the Santa Fe district schools offered Bailey more, he took it, which greatly saddened the community. Marion Douds, the respected high school principal, left for Denver that same year, after seventeen years in Dawson. Soon, Leroy Brannon, the coach and Douds's successor as principal, would leave, too, for Albuquerque. But good teachers also stayed, linked to the town by an intangible loyalty. Alice Devlin and Hannah McGarvey, who had been teaching in Dawson far longer than Bailey, each earned $1,602 in 1943. And that was fine with them.

Almost everyone who had the opportunity to teach in Dawson cherished the experience. Ruth Parker Shelton was twenty-two years old when she came to the town in 1928. She's never forgotten it: "In East Texas, my home, there were only two kinds of people: blacks and whites. I'd never seen any foreigners before. I'd never seen any Mexicans. So coming to Dawson was a revelation. I taught in junior high in Dawson, and I couldn't pronounce any names. I'd look at the roll and I'd see, say, 'Ralph Esquivel,' and I couldn't pronounce the last name. I'd say 'Ralph' . . . and nobody answered. Finally, someone said, 'That's not my name.' Then I'd try George Katsufrakis. I'd say, 'George'—'That's not my name,' he'd say.

"Oh, my. I got so depressed about all this that I would go home to the Teacherage at night and think about leaving. Then I'd think, 'What will Mama and Poppa think of me when I say I'm coming home?' You see, they had taught me to stay and finish what I started. So I did. By Christmas, I was happy in Dawson. I had recognized my limitations, and I would tell students, 'Say that name to me again.' Eventually, I learned how to pronounce their names, and my speech changed. They didn't change; I did."

Fenlon made graduating from high school an achievement, a feat as important as graduating from college. During Fenlon's first years in Dawson, few young people went on to college. But, as the schools got better and education was stressed more and more, that changed. Fenlon, who himself received an M.A. degree in history from the University of New Mexico while at Dawson, often went out of his way to seek scholarships for local students. Dawson schools thus turned out a fair number of doctors, dentists, attorneys, business leaders, and, not surprisingly, a slew of teachers who carried on the town's commitment to learning in classrooms across New Mexico and elsewhere. Pat Scanlon, who graduated from Dawson High School in 1949, and later had a successful career as a P.D. executive in New York City and Arizona, had the opportunity to attend

Harvard College. And it wouldn't have happened if Scanlon hadn't been doing his chores: "In a coal camp like Dawson, one of the heating chores was to empty the ashes from your coal stove. Our stove was in the kitchen, and one morning I pulled out the tray and spread the *Albuquerque Journal* beneath it to collect the fallen ashes. A headline in the newspaper caught my eye: 'Competitive Exams Scheduled for Harvard.' I stuffed the article in my pocket and that day showed it to my English teacher, Sara Miller. She encouraged me to apply for the Bronson Cutting National Scholarship, which went to one senior from New Mexico and Arizona.

"I was admitted and got the scholarship, and I suppose being from Dawson helped me. Leta Covert, one of my aunts, was the high school math teacher, and she made sure I took all the math that was available. And then there was Sara Miller, who made a big difference. She elevated my sights. She told us that we had a responsibility in life to do more than make good grades.

"The farthest east I had ever been was Oklahoma City, so when I got to Harvard it was a tremendous culture shock. But maybe for Harvard, too. In my freshman year, a college friend said to me, 'Are you going home to Mexico for Christmas?' Yes, I said, but to New Mexico. He said, 'What's the difference?' "

Since not many Dawsonites went to college, however, most remember their high school days as a high point in their young lives. Those were days of movies at the Opera House and dates at the Sweet Shop; of making a hatrack in Chester Pool's shop class; of studying Spanish with Dona Gail McWhirter or literature with Ann Komadina; of writing something crazy for the *Miner's Pick*; of wearing someone's big black cardigan letter sweater with the block red D on it; or of performing in

Douglas School, also known as Dawson High School, stood on one of the highest points in town.

The Mikado at the Opera House or singing the school song:

Oh Dawson High School; our dear old High School,
We'll be always true blue to you.
And there's no question in our minds of your superiority.
So we'll join forces and show the world
That we can reach the goal we seek
And climb the heights for our dear High School,
Then we'll Hail! All Hail!

Thanks to George Fenlon and the teachers he hired, Dawson received wide recognition when its high school became a member of the North Central Association of American Universities, a national accreditation organization, in 1924. Dawson was believed to be the only coal mining town in the United States to achieve such status. Fenlon himself gained acknowledgment of his achievements in 1932 when the National Education Association of New Mexico elected him president.

Apart from spending time with his wife and tending the

rose gardens that circled his house set back off Church Row, gardens that he often maintained in a suit and tie, Fenlon had few interests beyond his work. School systems across the country occasionally tried to lure the Professor away from Dawson, but, believing in the town and holding dear its people, he stayed put.

And yet, one of those people may inadvertently have been partly responsible for Fenlon's death. Always in good health because of his daily hikes to work, the superintendent in 1938 became bothered by an abscessed tooth. He visited Dawson's longtime dentist, Chester Hoover, a sweet soul but past his prime in terms of medical savvy. Hoover yanked the Professor's tooth, and an infection set in that likely caused other complications. Fenlon eventually was taken to the Mayo Clinic in Minnesota, where he died January 9, 1939.

Fenlon was only fifty-six when he was buried at Trinidad Catholic Cemetery in Colorado, yet he had served at Dawson for twenty-two years. ''The cause of education,'' eulogized P. K. Carson, secretary of Dawson's board of education and a venerable town official, ''has lost a great champion.'' School board members, faculty, and Phelps Dodge Corporation brass served as Fenlon's pallbearers. All of Dawson wept.

To George Fenlon, religion was just as necessary as education, and it rubbed off. Since the mines didn't run on Sunday, everybody in Dawson had time for church. Religion, like education, provided for young and old Dawsonites another means of unification, as well as significant values by which to live. Because of the hazardous nature of coal mining, prayer became a staple in most Dawson homes. And if you needed reminding about the nature of man's relationship to God, a clergyman usually was about. Indeed, a priest or Protestant pastor frequently was on hand for town-wide events, such as a football game, commencement, or a dance.

Any mention of religious life in Dawson must begin with Joseph Anthime Couturier. A French-Canadian member of the Oblates of Mary Immaculate, or OMI, Father Joseph, as he was known to all, served two tours as parish priest in Dawson, for a total of twenty-two years, and achieved, at times, saintly proportions.

The Archdiocese of Santa Fe had started a mission church in Dawson, answerable to the Springer parish, as early as 1915. Two years later, an arrangement was established with the Oblates, whose provincial headquarters were located in San Antonio, Texas, and a more formal congregation, as well as a church edifice, St. John the Baptist, first pastored by Couturier, were established. Founded in France in 1816, the OMI (''Ahblates'') was a missionary order that had come to Texas in 1849. ''He hath sent me to preach the gospel to the poor,'' was and still is the Oblate Fathers' creed. They preached in Texas and then expanded into Mexico, until the 1914 revolution there forced the Oblates north. In New Mexico's Colfax and Harding counties, the Oblates found a region of rich farmland and thriving coal camps. The OMI took over the church at Springer and made it their central parish for the area, forming parish churches in Roy and Dawson as well, plus many small missions in such places as Mills, Cimarron, Abbott, and Colmor.

In May 1917, the Archdiocese signed a contract with Phelps Dodge by which the company would furnish and maintain the Dawson church and rectory and supply free fuel, water, and electricity for $1 a year. In return, the Archdiocese guaranteed a priest in residence. During the 1920s, when Dawson reached its largest population of almost 8,000, the Oblates periodically had two priests in Dawson, Couturier and an associate. But there was never any doubt which man of the cloth was in charge.

Couturier arrived in Dawson on September 14, 1917, from a post in Del Rio, Texas. He was suffering from lung trouble and his health demanded the high, clear desert air. It was not easy being an Oblate at that time, healthy or not. In New Mexico they traveled about in a wheezing Ford nicknamed Angel Custodio, and they didn't always receive great receptions. In 1921, the Oblate in Roy was accused of having burned down the new public high school. Earlier, the priest had quarreled with the local Masons, and the school fire led that group to drag the poor father through the streets and subject him to insults and threats. Finally, after several hours in jail, the Oblate was released when it was learned that the contractor of the school had started the blaze. Nevertheless, the priest asked the local sheriff to accompany him everywhere, and soon the man was transferred back to Texas.

A slight man, darkly quiet and almost glum, Couturier nonetheless gained quick respect in Dawson by showing that he could speak Spanish and some Italian and Croatian as well. Yet at times he withdrew, stubbornly refusing to cross a line where he felt the church did not belong. For instance, in 1921 signs of the Ku Klux Klan briefly appeared, in response, it seemed, to Dawson's growing population of blacks and Catholics. For reasons of his own, Couturier did not address the Klan problem, and it later disappeared.

Despite his introverted, brooding nature, Couturier was revered by Dawson Catholics, particularly older ones, for his devoutness to God that manifested itself in a true dedication. Couturier comforted families during the hard times of mine strikes, and he was always around to deliver absolution follow-ing mine disasters. Whenever a mine accident occurred, Couturier insisted upon going underground to be with the injured. So committed was Couturier to Dawson, so afraid that a cave-in might take place in his absence, that the priest did not even like to leave town to take a meal in Springer with the other OMI fathers. If Couturier had one message to give to his flock, it was this: a miner who goes to work in the morning might not come back at night. Thus, he implored families to pray, and to say novenas and rosaries, and to observe significant holy days, such as St. John the Baptist Day on June 24, or El Dia de los Muertos on November 2, or the Feast of Guadalupe Day on December 12. Couturier also served as chaplain to Dawson's hospital, and he was on hand for wakes. Because Dawson did not have a funeral home—only a morgue—when a Catholic died there would often be a vigil at home, followed by a Mass at church. Countless were the times when Father Joseph, standing sympathetically in a Dawsonite's living room, warmed by a coal stove, would calm a hysterical wife or mother.

St. John the Baptist—a sturdy, stone building with simple crosses atop its three façades, and an imposing and steep flight of steps out front and concrete-hard pews within—was one of the few buildings in Dawson not built by Phelps Dodge. Mass at St. John the Baptist was held daily, at 6:00 A.M., though most worshippers didn't go to the church until the 8:30 service on Sunday mornings. At 10:30 A.M. on Sundays another service was held there, known as the Mexican Mass. Both the sermon and music at the second service were in Spanish.

Though Dawson held Couturier in high regard, the veteran priest could be a hard-liner in those days of preliberal Catholicism. If a youth were Hispanic, for instance, Couturier forced him to take catechism in Spanish, instead of English.

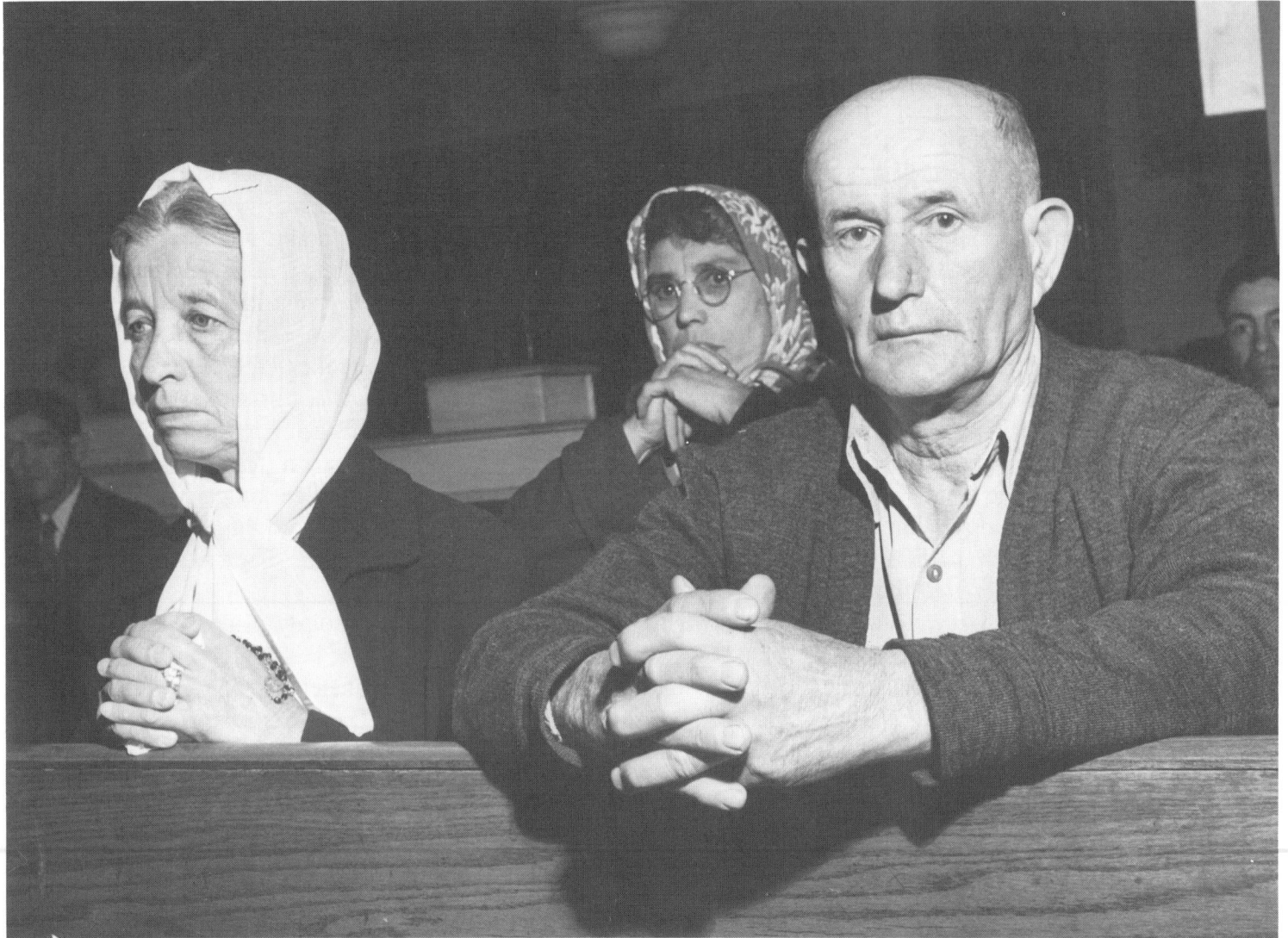

Dawson Catholics found comfort at St. John the Baptist Church.

If a youthful member of St. John the Baptist were invited to, say, a church supper at the Community Church, the only other place of worship in town and located just around the corner, Couturier did not like it, and said so. Couturier was known to pull kids out of the Opera House to attend a church function, and he did not spare a pencil to the head or even a slap if a young person forgot his lessons.

But for most of the Catholics in Dawson, Couturier was someone to be followed—on occasions such as the special Thanksgiving Mass, the Immaculate Conception Day on December 8, the Easter processions, and during the month of May when devotions to Mary filled St. John the Baptist with the scent of plum blossoms. Over the years, Couturier christened hundreds of Dawson babies and served most of them their first Holy Communion. If those children stayed on in town, Couturier was around to marry them and, quite possibly, bury them. The priest even taught some parishioners how to play the pipe organ.

Dawsonites repaid Couturier by working in the church, inviting him home for a meal, or by merely attending church regularly. Of course, some appeared at St. John the Baptist only on Christmas Eve. But for those who kneeled during a midnight Mass that evening, who smelled the incense and felt the warmth of the candles and gazed at the stations of the cross and the statues, and who, finally, sang "O Holy Night," it was an experience that could last well into the following year.

Perhaps altar boys loved Father Joseph most of all. Yes, the priest made sure the sons of Victor Padilla and Terence Scanlon and Clemente Di Domenico had cleaned their uniforms and had memorized their Latin prayers. But at Christmastime, Couturier would split the contents of the collection plate with his helpers, some years giving his charges as much as $5 each.

St. John the Baptist Church was located at a prominent spot on Main Street.

Joseph "Jiggy" Palumbo never served as an altar boy, but he had attended St. John the Baptist from almost the day he was born in 1913. When Palumbo died in 1936, at age twenty-three, cut down one Sunday afternoon in July by a lightning bolt on a baseball diamond in Raton, it would cause a deep religious rift in Dawson.

Palumbo was an enormously friendly young man who came from a large and well-liked family. He had wanted to be a coach after high school, but, with no jobs available, he went into the mines and soon became a union organizer. An athlete, Palumbo had wavy-haired good looks and a laugh that never seemed to cease. Indeed, he was laughing as he ran across the infield to his spot at second base on the afternoon lightning

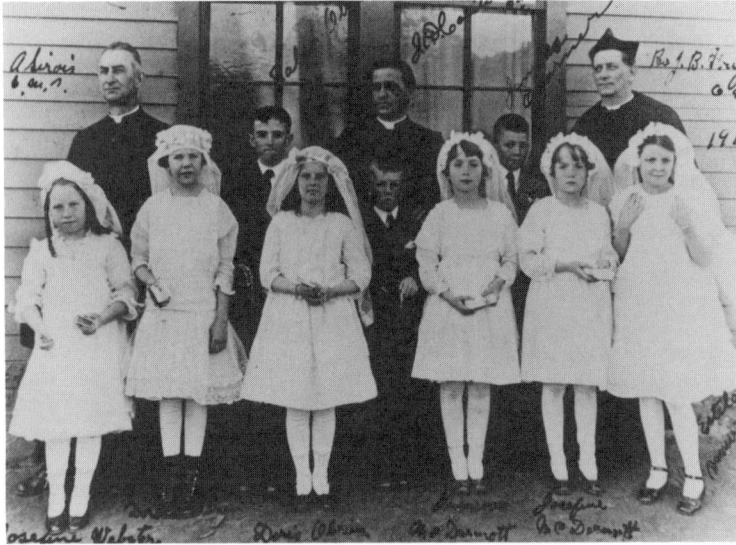

For young Catholics in Dawson,
First Communion was a special day.

shredded his ball cap. Palumbo's death shocked the town, not just because he died so young, but because he died doing what Dawsonites believed to be sacrosanct: playing sports. And yet the real shock occurred afterward. Because Jiggy Palumbo had married Leola Meikle, a Protestant, and had gone off to Taos to tie the knot in front of a justice of the peace, and because Palumbo had not received the last sacraments when he died, Couturier refused to hold the young man's Mass. Nor did the priest permit Palumbo to be buried in the Catholic section of the Dawson cemetery, alongside his mother, who only four months before at the age of forty-eight had died of pneumonia. Palumbo had been extremely close to his mother; on the morning that he died, he had told his family to be sure to put flowers on her grave.

Eventually, a funeral was held for Palumbo at the Community Church, and the service drew one of the biggest crowds that Dawson had ever seen. Everyone came, it seemed, except Father Joseph.

Less than a year later, the Oblates transferred Couturier to Louisiana. Some believe it was because of criticism Dawsonites directed at the Archdiocese of Santa Fe over the handling of the Jiggy Palumbo incident. Indeed, later that summer of 1936, the archbishop visited the town in what surely was meant as a conciliatory call. But Couturier, after nineteen years in Dawson, was tired, and may have been experiencing the beginnings of a breakdown. Three months after Palumbo died, Couturier wrote this to OMI officials in San Antonio: "I don't feel like I can continue without having a little rest . . . I am sure the people will appreciate the change, because the new man will be different, and will put more life in the parish. For sometime I am very nervous, and cannot do as I should do, so, before I am altogether down, I come to ask you this favor, that is to remove me from the high altitude for a few years, and give me a chance to recuperate, be myself again."

Dawson's new man *was* different. Gustav Gollbach was an outgoing, cultured German, a lover of art and chess, an OMI who, in his early days of the priesthood in Texas, traveled miles and miles by horseback. Legend had it that Gollbach once outrode one of Buffalo Bill's Indian scouts.

Gollbach was fifty-nine when he arrived in Dawson in 1937, and he no longer rode horses. In fact, he had slowed down considerably. During that first year in town, the new priest, standing at the altar of St. John the Baptist one Sunday morning, suddenly clutched his chest and then fell to the floor, the victim of a heart attack. One of the first parishioners to reach the fallen priest, and the person who may have saved

Gollbach's life, was, ironically, Domenico Palumbo, Jiggy's father. The senior Palumbo had been so grief-stricken by his son's death and the subsequent furor it caused, happening so soon after his wife's passing, that he had refused to let the family hold a wake. On top of that, Domenico Palumbo had stayed away from church for a good long time and had only returned when a new priest took over.

For some Dawsonites, religious experiences were so joyful and profound that they influenced the direction of a life's course. Mary Frances García Reza grew up in St. John the Baptist. Her mother played the organ there, and later she took that job. Mary Frances sang in the Hispanic choir, and that's where she met her husband, Henry. Finally, Mary Frances became choir director, work that provided her with a foundation for everything she does now, which is to serve as director for the Office of Worship for the Archdiocese of Santa Fe. Reza gives workshops all over the country on Spanish music and culture, and she was instrumental in helping publish one of the largest Spanish hymnals in existence.

Michael Cimino was ten years old and living in Dawson when he experienced his moment of epiphany. "My mother had contracted double pneumonia and was near death. Father Joseph came to our house on Capitan, and I can remember him coming with the blessed sacraments and oils. Father Joseph held confession for my mother, and then he led me and my four sisters into the bedroom. My father that day was working in the mines. In Latin, Father Joseph gave the blessing to my mother: he blessed her forehead and extremities, and then he used the oils. He'd dip his thumb into the oil, and, still speaking in Latin, he touched her on the forehead, hands, and feet. We spoke Italian at home, so I understood some of the Latin. Because my mother lived, it was a special

Protestants in Dawson attended the Community Church.

time for me, a moment that I think later made me wish to serve God." Today, Cimino is an Albuquerque priest.

The history of the nondenominational Community Church is not as indelible as that of St. John the Baptist's, surely because there were far fewer Protestants than Catholics in Dawson. Phelps Dodge certainly supported the Community Church—James Douglas, the corporation president and a staunch Presbyterian, had gifted the town with a Protestant chapel, among the first public buildings erected in the town.

In its very early days, the Community Church was served by Harvey Shields, an Episcopalian. Then, for almost twenty-six years, Joseph S. Russel, a lanky, mustachioed ex-Baptist, originally from New Jersey, led the congregation. Russel first came to New Mexico in 1908 to work in the home mission field in Roy, as a Presbyterian, his new denomination. He settled in Dawson in 1915 and, for the next quarter century, lived quietly next door to the Community Church in a parsonage with his wife, Henrietta. Not an especially dynamic preacher —Russel recycled his sermons yearly and lectured schoolchildren at every opportunity on the stuporous topic of "The Value of Education"—the minister earned an enduring place in the hearts of Dawsonites in 1923. Summoned to Mine Number One on a Thursday afternoon in February of that year, Russel arrived to identify the body of his son-in-law, Robert Holmes, one of 120 men killed in Dawson's second worst mining disaster.

Despite their theological differences, Russel and Couturier became good friends. Like Couturier, Russel was a reserved man who had a great fondness for Dawson. Indeed, the two worked side by side to offer comfort in the aftermath of the 1923 explosion. And it was Russel who conducted Jiggy Palumbo's funeral service.

Russel surely must have understood early on that the Community Church would always be of secondary importance in Dawson. Though it had given name to the well-trod Dawson street of Church Row, where it was located, compared to St. John the Baptist, the Community Church was small. Its sanctuary could fit inside the Catholic church's, and its morning service was no match for St. John the Baptist's well-attended Mexican Mass, held at the same time. Still, the Community Church featured a well-attended Sunday evening vesper service.

A low-slung building topped by a prominent bell tower, the Community Church contained two classrooms located off the sides of the sanctuary where Sunday School was taught. The Sunday School—largest of any coal town in the West—was the focal point of Protestant life in Dawson because of one person: Hannah McGarvey. As strong a Christian as she was an educator, McGarvey brought the Bible to life for at least two generations of Dawsonites. And when J. S. Russel became

ill—in failing health for some time, he died in Las Vegas, New Mexico, in 1941 at age eighty-one—McGarvey filled in. McGarvey felt so strongly about her faith that she thought nothing of standing in her yard on Saturday mornings and yelling to neighborhood boys, "I'll see you in Sunday School tomorrow, won't I?" McGarvey wasn't the only pillar of the Community Church in her family. Her brother-in-law, J. F. McClary, served for many years as the church's choir director, though he could not read a note of music.

In 1945, a recuperated Joseph Couturier made a triumphal return to Dawson. He had requested a reassignment to the town, and any ill feelings about him were put aside, for Dawsonites are quick to recognize one of their own, and quick to forgive. Moreover, there had begun to exist in the community a real feeling that the town was dying. Father Joseph's presence, like the return of a long lost friend, seemed to allay those fears of doom.

During this last stay in Dawson, Couturier served as the superior of the Oblate fathers in the Springer District. But he was heavier now, and hiking up Dawson's hills or traveling to outlying missions in another clunking Ford owned by the order sometimes seemed more than the old priest could manage. In the fall of 1948, Couturier became ill, and on October 26 of that year he died of pneumonia in Mount San Rafael Hospital in Trinidad, Colorado, at age sixty-seven. After lying in state in St. John the Baptist, the priest's body was to be taken to San Antonio, Texas, for burial in the Oblate Fathers cemetery there. As a hearse slowly made its way down Main Street toward Dawson's depot, the whole town, it seemed, walked behind. And, as they had for George Fenlon, the whole town wept.

Chapter Seven

COMPETING

"Everybody there was raised to play sports and to win."

—Pat Rainwater

At age eighty, Virgil Saracino still has the build of a Russian war memorial. His shoulders stretch across an archway, his chest swells like a nail keg, his forearms nearly equal the circumference of fireplace logs. Even his eyebrows, great black caterpillars that wriggle over his dark face, look strong. When he lived in Dawson, Saracino operated a steam shovel, which seems fitting for someone so physically imposing. It also seems appropriate that Saracino should be considered the greatest athlete in a town that scooped out a large and holy place in its heart for sports. "I don't want to brag," growls Saracino in a voice that resembles a foghorn in foul weather, "but I could make fifteen, eighteen tackles in a football game and nobody would know. I punted a ball eighty-five yards and nobody cared. See, in them days, you didn't get many write-ups."

"Them days" were the early 1930s. Standing five feet ten inches and weighing 175 pounds, Saracino was thought of as a giant for his time, and in the tradition of the illustrious Bronco Nagurski he played fullback and linebacker. More than anything, however, Saracino epitomized the toughness that became synonymous with the Dawson Miner.

A kid in Dawson had to be tough. If your father worked in the mine, as Joe Saracino did, he couldn't hand over to you an allowance every week or the keys to the car. Instead, if you were young Verge, you played sports from the time you could totter. At first, sandlot sports. Want a football? Use that two-quart milk can. A baseball bat? Here, take this big oak club, the one that a mine hand whittled from a motor pole. A field to play on? Go over to that bare area across the way, the spot with more rocks than a riverbed. "Not too many Dawson kids," says Saracino, "were pampered."

But why the passion for sports? Several reasons. Sports, Phelps Dodge realized, was a way to unify the town and keep workers happy. "Every possible encouragement," explained the *Dawson News,* "is given to those phases of social activities making for the contentment and well-being of her cosmopolitan population." In 1926, the corporation built an eight-foot-deep swimming pool west of downtown, a complex that featured a diving board, locker rooms, and surely one of the first water slides in the Southwest. Two tennis courts were laid down nearby during that same period, and Phelps Dodge was forever pushing swimming races and tennis tournaments—the P. G. Beckett Cup in tennis was named for a high-ranking company official. Phelps Dodge encouraged residents to take part in other sports as well. "They put you on a team," says Pat Rainwater, "whether you wanted to be on it or not." You could join one of the eight teams in the town bowling league that rolled in the two lanes in the basement of the Opera House. Or you could be a member of the walking club, an organization designed for, said the *Dawson News,* "the pleasantly plump." There were softball teams sponsored by the barbershop and the machine shop. A soccer squad, composed mainly of Welsh miners, achieved notoriety when, after a game with Sugarite, tea was served to all players. Some civilized soul even organized a croquet club.

There were inherent reasons why Dawson High School usually was vying for a district championship. Though nobody lifted weights, sinew was passed down from fathers and grandfathers whose torsos had been built up from doing manual labor. Additionally, Dawson's youth got plenty of exercise just walking up the steep hills around town. When Fred Bergamo finished football practice, he faced a two-mile hike, most of it uphill, and all of it in the dark, to get home. Nick Gonzáles, another football player, hoofed—sometimes he even ran—a mile and a half to high school each day, even in the snow, for in Dawson there was no such thing as a snow day. Also, young people in town generally ate well. Even kids from large families who didn't get a lot of food got the right kinds, for just about everyone in the community had a garden. Finally, Dawson athletes were mature. Many, unable to speak English, spent a year or more learning the language in a special program before finally enrolling in public school at age seven. Thus, it wasn't unusual for Dawson High to have nineteen-year-old, even twenty-year-old seniors.

The town's athletic success was based on more than stamina, diet, or maturity, however. A community spirit motivated Dawson's sports teams. Dawson was a proud place, and living there—with the reminders of two terrible mining disasters and the daily threat of another—taught people how to endure in the face of danger. And yet living there also made Dawsonites want to show others that the town could be known for something besides cave-ins. Community spirit meant competing against a neighboring coal mining camp, like Swastika or Brilliant or Van Houten, and beating it senseless. Community spirit also meant supporting your team, for spectating offered great relief from the worries and exhaustion of coal mining. Surely the high point of town ardor occurred in 1923. The mine explosion that killed more than 120 men on Feb-

*The 1937 football team, with Coach P.G. Flood (front row far left),
had an 8–0 record and shared a state championship.*

ruary 8 of that year caused a basketball game with Springer to be canceled the day following the tragedy. There was talk of abandoning the entire season, but on February 16 school officials decided to ''carry on,'' as someone put it, and play a scheduled game with Raton, a contest that would decide the conference championship. Dawson's hesitancy to play had been intensified because Fred English, a star forward on the team, had lost his father and brother in the disaster. Somehow, however, English found the will to accompany the team to Raton, where he unfortunately experienced more heartbreak: the Dawson boys lost by just two points.

Mining coal calls for teamwork. In Dawson, that ability to get along, that trust, transferred aboveground to the town's picnics and dances and particularly to its athletic teams, whose members went to school and church together, fished, hunted, and double-dated together, and, finally, passed the ball to one another. It is no wonder that, while Dawson turned out few great athletes in individual sports, its teams—football, basketball, and baseball—were usually first-class.

Sports involved the entire town. A football game in the community caused a merchant such as shoe repairman Oresto Di Cianno to close his shop for the day. Many businesspeople, in fact, shut down even for away games. The *Dawson News* of July 27, 1922 noted: ''Almost all the people of Dawson attended the baseball game at Trinidad Sunday.'' To get to out-of-town games in the days before most Dawsonites had cars, young and old would wait down at the Phelps Dodge Conoco station that Bob Easley ran until somebody pulled up in a coupe and offered a ride.

Camps within Dawson—Number Seven, Old Capitan, Loreta—fielded athletic teams in the early days, as did specific mines. Foremen had teams, too, and so did the Boy Scouts,

and saloons such as Trani's and Bocho's. The latter even had a league for boccie players. When cars became more prevalent in Dawson, townspeople would drive down to the ballpark along the entrance road, rim the outfield with the noses of their Packards, and honk when someone such as Virgil Saracino hit a home run. As darkness crept in, fans would turn on their headlights.

Dawsonites had just as much interest in national sports as local sports. In the days before radios were commonplace, a good crowd would be on hand to watch Harry Fisher, the Southern Pacific telegraph agent, post the score of a World Series game on a blackboard in the depot. And just as many people would hang around the Phelps Dodge Mercantile to listen to Series games broadcast through the store's big loudspeakers. Even if you were working underground, you got the news: a World Series scoreboard was chalked to the side of a pit car and then sent through the mine.

Dawson was wild about sports long before Verge Saracino came along. In the town's early days ''basket ball''—and that's how they spelled it—was played on the stage of the Opera House, with half of the gate receipts going to the rental of the ornate building. There the Minerettes, the Dawson girls basketball team, who wore sailor suits, once shut out Maxwell, 32-0. As dramatic as perspiring in the Opera House might have seemed, a new location was sorely needed, as editorials in the *Dawson News* constantly urged. When the original company store was remodeled in 1922, Dawson acquired its first real gym, where teams would play for nearly thirty years.

The Dawson Gymnasium's location—adjacent to the busy, new P.D. Mercantile, just inside the gateway to town—signaled the importance of sports in the community. However, it was so small and confined that players, almost always those from

At one time the company store, the gymnasium served as an intimate arena for the town's basketball fortunes.

other teams, frequently crashed into the brick walls of the building, or onto the potbellied stove in the corner, or against the pillars that stood just out-of-bounds and held up the balcony. In that balcony, where spectators perched on folding chairs, it was not unusual to see an excited Dawson rooter lean over and reach down toward the court to bat the ball out of the air as it traveled toward a basket, almost always the other team's. Because opponents never really got used to Dawson's gym, their fans often chanted the following during games:

> We're no chickens,
> We're no fox,
> We can't play
> In this crackerbox.

Dawsonites, even immigrants who had never seen the game, poured into the crackerbox gym. Community spirit was so pervasive that often the entire front page of the *Dawson News* was given over to the results of a basketball game, reports that sometimes quaintly referred to players only by their first names.

Records show Dawson High School had basketball, track, and baseball teams as far back as 1917, though competition was mostly informal. The Dawson class of 1919 did have two fine athletes in Cullen Pearce and Fred Covert, but Dawson teams of those days were not outstanding. In 1921, the Miners, wearing long pants and sleeveless jerseys, and coached by school superintendent George Fenlon, were asked to play in the boy's state basketball tournament in Albuquerque. The team had not won a game all year, but the town was so flattered by the invitation that it raised money to send the young men on "the long, hard trip." Dawson lost in the first round to Menaul School, 22-19, and thus finished its year winless.

Over time, of course, the high school's basketball team improved. In 1925, the Miners beat Dawson's town team, as well as archrival Raton, coached by Charles B. Sweeney, a man who for years stood as a nemesis among Dawson fans. As codistrict champions that year, the Miners took that long, hard trip to Albuquerque and the state tournament, where they lost to Menaul again. "A splendid showing," reported the *Dawson News*, summoning a favorite phrase. A curious footnote to that event was also reported in the *DN:* "Judge Gavin was so pleased with the basketball game Saturday night that he gave the winning team five dollars." The following year the Dawson boys posted a 17-2 record and declared themselves northern New Mexico champions. The 10-1 victory of the girls' team, coached by schoolteacher Alberta McGarvey, caused the *Dawson News* to gush, "They can easily be classed with the best teams in the state."

When basketball moved out of the Opera House, it did not spell the end of athletic events in that grand structure. Wrestling exhibitions on the stage regularly featured local

Dawson's 1918 basketball team, coached by Superintendent George Fenlon, was like many school teams: short on numbers but long on heart.

strongmen, such as George Gustovich, who tangled for an hour and a half with a slab of beef named Zbyszko. When Emil Dominik, the New Mexico lightweight wrestling champion, went against G. E. Richards of Colorado, the competition nearly caused a riot in the Opera House. "Battling Billy Burns" or Marnie Galvan or wiry little Jesús Montalvo, from Number One Camp, frequently took to the stage to put on boxing demonstrations. Those events and others were sanctioned by the Dawson Club, a council that organized and promoted many of the town's sporting activities. Of particular interest to the Dawson Club was the formation and management of the town's baseball and basketball teams, squads usually made up of older players who competed against other town teams in New Mexico and Colorado.

Baseball in Dawson started in high school in 1920, and the following year the Miners played a single game with Raton. "We expect to win it," announced *Ye Coke Breeze*. But high school baseball always took second place to the town team. Springtime in Dawson was often too windy for much baseball, and as summer approached and it was less windy, the town baseball team, called variously the Miners, Merchants, or Indians, took the spotlight.

The town baseball team—at one point Dawson had two teams—provided athletes with an opportunity to compete after they left high school. In fact, when Virgil Saracino was in his mid-thirties, he was still playing catcher for Dawson. Games took place on the field on the road into town. "We always had a full house," remembers Saracino. "But in Trinidad or Raton, you had very few people there come out." On one occasion, when the town team played in El Paso, Dawsonites chartered an entire Pullman car to accompany the players. There was a great deal of pride at stake in these games, so much that Phelps Dodge was not above hiring men only if they were proficient at baseball. Fritz Koelling, who came to Dawson in the 1920s but found little work available suddenly got a job when the company discovered Koelling played catcher. The Stag Cañon Branch even recruited baseball talent from out of state, promising an undemanding job in the carpentry shop or the washery. This arrangement worked well until one year a pitcher, a professional prospect some said, was brought from Denver and given the task of watching over a

Some of the best seats at the ball field were the front seat of a Ford.

Even those deep in Dawson's mines needed to know the score of a World Series game.

simple piece of machinery; the recruit caught his right arm, the one he pitched with, in the mechanism.

Town team games were lively affairs, and few spectators sitting in the ballpark's big, wood-covered grandstand could keep silent for long. Perhaps the loudest fan was a black laborer named Redo Simmons, who led rousing cheers. As usual, games were exhaustively reported in the *Dawson News,* along with colorful editorial commentary such as the following: ''If Jimmy could heave coal like he does a baseball, Number Three Mine would break all production records in short order.'' Good sportsmanship was expected, for P.D. would not tolerate otherwise. Usually one of the community's more well-respected citizens, such as a priest, was called on to umpire, and seldom was his judgment questioned. Once, during a game with Trinidad, the visitors were charged with doctoring a baseball. The umpire on hand removed the ball in question and later placed it on public display in the barbershop.

Football had an inglorious beginning in Dawson. In the high school's first game on October 7, 1922, the Miners lost to Trinidad, 82-0. Trinidad, the *Dawson News* politely pointed out, ''was familiar with the rudiments of the game.'' Dawson scored a total of 13 points that year, getting swamped twice by Raton, while its opponents scored 232 points. Bill Saul, who played defensive lineman and running back, says, ''Nobody had ever seen a football game, let alone played one.'' Saul, at 140 pounds, was one of the biggest players on the team. The coach, a fellow named Hemphill, soon left, perhaps out of despondency. He was replaced by Woody Holmes, an enthusiastic young graduate of the University of Illinois. But Holmes struggled, too. In 1925, his Miners won no games and lost to Raton, 41-0. A couple of years later Dawson got whipped by Des Moines, 55-0, then fell to Raton, 46-7. Why the losses?

Saul says too many of Dawson's young men were going into the mines or getting married while still in high school; also Dawson players were small and lacked knowledge of football. Fans, however, continued to turn out for games in good numbers, and the *Dawson News* never ceased to backslap the splendid work done by "our boys."

Certainly Dawson was not without talent. Carlyle Vickers, a fullback of the 1920s, went on to play football for Colorado Agricultural College, now Colorado State, and even appeared in the East-West Shrine Game, made up of the country's top college seniors. Still, the losses kept mounting. "I was just a real young kid," says Saracino, "but I remember how awful those teams were. They always talked about how friendly Clayton was to Dawson. That's not how to play football!"

As Dawson's football teams got worse and rival Raton's got better, a new coach was obviously needed. The man hired was Harry Brydon, an assistant at Trinidad, a small, red-complected drill sergeant everyone called "Pinky." The next season the Miners won their first four football games, all by shutouts. Loud and forceful, Pinky Brydon introduced tackling dummies to Dawson, and when the team didn't use them correctly the coach stopped practice and tackled players himself.

Despite his success, Brydon lasted only a year at Dawson. His problem? As a married man, he committed the unpardonable sin, at least as far as straitlaced George Fenlon was concerned, of chasing after a female schoolteacher. Once again Dawson went looking for a coach who knew how to win and wouldn't cause embarrassment. Fenlon found him in Paul Gosney Flood, who was twenty-six when he came to Dawson in the summer of 1929. Like Holmes, P. G. Flood had graduated from Illinois, and the Midwest-rooted Fenlon liked that. Flood had taught some in Blackwell, Oklahoma, where he was born and grew up, but his chief experience had come from watching others. At Illinois, Flood had been a student with the immortal Red Grange and had carefully followed the fortunes of the "Galloping Ghost" and his coach, Bob Zuppke. When Flood first appeared in Dawson, he wore a dark blue cardigan sweater with an orange "I" on it. All Dawsonites assumed that the new coach had played football for the Illini. But he hadn't. Curiously, Flood, short and sturdy, had been a college wrestler.

Firm of jaw and direct of gaze, Flood definitely was a winner. In fact, in his first year at Dawson the Miners went 9-0. The next year the team was 6-1-1. Though townspeople took notice of those statistics, newspaper polls, at the time the only public judge of a team's worth, scarcely paid attention. Dawson, after all, played small, insignificant schools such as Kiowa and Grenville, and larger schools such as Raton always got the ink. Therefore nobody knew of Verge Saracino's eighteen tackles or of his eighty-five-yard punts.

In some respects, Raton deserved the publicity. The Tigers won a state basketball championship in 1929, Flood's first year, and they were just as good in football. Indeed, Dawson had developed a complex about Raton, believing the Tigers were so much bigger physically that they should win. This fact was forever engraved on Dawsonites' brains the day the two teams played a football game and a Dawson player, a pint-sized kid, scurried with the ball between a Raton player's legs.

To help the Miners gain stature in the football polls and experience on the field, Flood scheduled games against powerhouses from Pueblo, Colorado, Albuquerque, and Clovis. He'd then follow a big school with a pushover like Aguilar, Colorado. Finally, he saved the Raton game for Thanksgiving Day, and geared Dawson's season toward that event. At the same time, though, Flood continually reminded players like Saracino that Dawson kids were as tough as anybody, probably tougher, just by the nature of their backgrounds.

The first time a Flood-coached team met Raton, in 1930, the Miners lost, but only by a touchdown. In five out of the next seven years, however, Dawson had the edge and beat a lot of other teams as well. "Clayton wasn't friendly to us anymore," says Saracino. "We were kicking the heck out of 'em now."

The Flood juggernaut truly got rolling in 1931 and 1932, Saracino's junior and senior seasons. "How good were we?" asks Saracino. "We went two years and hardly anybody scored any touchdowns on us." Indeed, the Miners crushed everyone in their path: Dawson 88, Cimarron 0; Dawson 86, Maxwell 0. Sportswriters suddenly began to take notice.

Saracino carried the "moleskin" a lot for Dawson. He played football for five years and lettered in all five. In fact, he never was out of a game and never got hurt. "A coach from another town asked me once, 'When are you going to graduate?' " In a rare write-up, the *Raton Range* said "In Verge Saracino Miner supporters believe they have the best fullback in the state."

Saracino and Flood developed an unusual relationship. When the new coach arrived in Dawson, Saracino was only a ninth grader, but when Flood saw how durable he was he never substituted Saracino. After Saracino's sophomore year, his family moved to Utah, where Joe Saracino took a new job. "I wanted to stay in Dawson," says Virgil, "and coach Flood wanted me there. So one night he comes up to the house and talks to my sister. My mother had died. Coach Flood told her he wanted me in town. Coach Flood talked me into

staying with John Venetti, a bachelor and truck farmer who worked in Dawson. Venetti said I could live with him and pay room and board. So that's what I done my last three years of high school. I guess you could say then that Coach Flood recruited me."

Wearing flimsy shoulder pads and cardboard helmets during the 1930s, Dawson gained a reputation as a smart team that would never quit. Says Saracino: "Joe Colombo, one of our linemen, weighed maybe 118 pounds. But nobody went around him." And Flood gained a reputation as a coach whose players would do anything for him: one young man played the whole second half of a game with a broken collarbone. Unlike Pinky Brydon, Flood wasn't loud, but he had a way of making his point. When a Dawson fan yelled from the sidelines too much to suit the coach, Flood, in the middle of the game, would go over, grab the spectator by the neck, and firmly tell him to stop.

State football championships weren't officially recognized in New Mexico until the 1950s, but in 1937 Dawson, with an 8-0 record under Flood, is credited with sharing the title with four other teams. Although Saracino was gone by then, making Tony De La Luz at 168 pounds the heaviest Miner, the team made up for a lack of size with many hammer-hard players, among them John Jackovich, Dally Lancieri, George Skandale, and George Katsufrakis. Quarterback George Gustovich could hurl a football sixty yards, and Mike "Snake" Carlini drop-kicked one forty-two yards, the first and last field goal of his life, to beat Clovis and their legendary coach Rock Staubus, 10-6, in 1938. That contest, held in Clovis for the early-season right to be called best team in the state, was one of the first high school games in New Mexico played at night.

The years 1937 and 1938 were banner ones for Flood. The

Thanksgiving Day classic in 1937 attracted 2,500 fans to Raton's Legion Field. Going into the game, Dawson was undefeated, and Raton had only one tie to mar its record. The outsized Miners won, 19-0. "A spectacular tilt," marveled the *Raton Daily Range.* However, the following Thanksgiving in Dawson, Raton reversed things, winning 19-0 and becoming state champs.

Dawson's fondness for football did not extend to everyone. Nick Di Domenico, like most boys in Dawson, wanted to play football badly, but his father wouldn't let him. Clemente Di Domenico, a coal-loader by profession, not only didn't understand football, he thought sports were a waste of time. "Papa said we ought to work," says Nick. "So I pulled weeds for ten cents an hour." Finally, when he couldn't stand it anymore, Nick, only 132 pounds, sneaked out of his house every day to play for P. G. Flood.

Whether one played or not, a magnetism surrounded Dawson football. Before home games, a parade formed along Main Street. And when the team went on the road, trips often financed by Phelps Dodge, the marching band went along, a rarity among high schools in those days. Since many miners' families could not afford the extra expense, and youngsters had few opportunities to travel, Herbert Bailey, the longtime, astute band director, insisted on taking them.

Cheerleading was also part of the pageantry. "We wore scandalous outfits," says Grayce Padilla Britton. "Short skirts and little sweaters with a D on them. Red and black colors, of course. We carried red and black megaphones, too." Britton became a cheerleader in the tenth grade. "You didn't have any tryouts like you do today. We just went out there and cheered, like everybody else in town. Me and Dorothy Carlini. What did we cheer?

Give me an M
Give me an I
Give me an N
Give me an E
Give me an R
Give me an S
Yea, Miners!

Cheered on, P. G. Flood's teams began to excel in basketball as they did in football. With Verge Saracino wearing suction-cup knee pads and shorts with a belt, and jumping center after every basket, the Miners usually did well in the prestigious Cowbell Tournament, a regional event that awarded the winner a big bronze cowbell. By beating such teams as the Springer Red Devils and the Cimarron Rams, Dawson made local heroes out of Jimmy Herrera, Kayo Frani, Allen Moore, Rodolfo Ghiglieri, and the Ragni brothers. Though Flood wasn't as captivated by basketball as by football, he nonetheless brought the Miners to the state tournament eight times. (In all, Dawson went to state a remarkable twelve times, as many as any team during its existence except Albuquerque High.) In 1943, the Miners, led by gangly center Roy Rork, missed getting into the state championship game by two points and wound up in third place among all teams, their best finish ever in basketball.

In his fourteen years at Dawson, Flood's teams won almost 100 football games; they totaled nearly six times as many points as their opponents. But Flood was more than a man who racked up glittering statistics. "He never cut a boy," says Di Domenico. "Coach Flood didn't believe in it. You cut your ownself." He treated second and third stringers in Dawson so well that they called themselves "rinky dinks"—with respect.

Flood's fairness knew no ethnic bounds, which in Dawson was not always easy. Says Di Domenico: "Flood didn't move people around or say, 'He's an Italian, so he'll play there, or you're a German, so you play there.' "

Flood didn't let the victories get in the way of what he felt was right. Among other things he didn't allow any cussing or drinking on his teams. When the coach found out a star member of the football team had been drinking beer, he gave the boy the boot, even when Flood's daughter begged her father not to. Flood handed out the same punishment to a first-string tackle whom the coach had caught smoking. Conversely, as a history teacher in the high school, Flood was said to give A's to any athlete.

Even outside of school, sports consumed Dawson's coach. He usually stayed in town in the summer to manage the swimming pool, where he liked to keep the water at a chilly sixty-five degrees. Or he'd take his family back to the Midwest, where he liked to watch the St. Louis Cardinals play baseball. At home, Flood was considered a kind and gentle father. "But we had to be very quiet and out of the way when he was working with all those *X*'s and *O*'s," says Anita Brown, his daughter. "He loved all his teams and the players. I think they were as much his children as we were. When the season was over, he always invited the teams over to our house for a spaghetti dinner."

Flood's wife gave birth to four children in Dawson. However, she died while delivering the fourth, leaving the young coach to raise the brood by himself, a fact that gained Flood further admiration in town. Flood later married Kathleen Henry, a pretty, young widow who had been born in Dawson and had gone on to be named Homecoming Queen at the University of New Mexico at age fourteen. Outwardly, things seemed fine,

until Flood announced in 1943 that he had accepted a job in Clayton. Flood would be getting more money in Clayton, but the coach also left because his marriage was in trouble. A dashing figure, Flood found himself with numerous female admirers. Though the coach never caused embarrassment, rumors began to fly until finally the school superintendent, as his predecessor had done with Pinky Brydon, encouraged Flood to move on.

Flood did not have the success in Clayton that he had had in Dawson. "I asked him why once," says Saracino. "He said, 'The kids in Dawson wanted to play football. The kids in Clayton wanted to play at it.' "

Flood's troubled second marriage fell apart in Clayton, and the couple divorced. He remarried there in 1947, stayed on for a few years, and then moved to Oregon, where he taught and coached. Flood came back briefly to New Mexico in the 1960s and taught at Española, in order to finish out a state retirement requirement, returning afterward to the Northwest, where he died in Astoria, Oregon, in 1974 at age seventy-one. "The most dedicated man I knew," says Saracino. "His word was law. I think he eased up at the end, but I know being that strict influenced me. I wanted to be a coach like him, but I never made it."

Nor did Saracino ever become a golfer, despite the fact that golf was also popular in Dawson. "The game didn't appeal to me," he says, and his tone is unmistakable: golf is for the pampered. Phelps Dodge put in the first golf course in 1912, atop Capitan, making it one of the oldest golf links in New Mexico. In 1921, when the high school was built on the hill, the golf course was moved to an area west of town known as Lacy Canyon. Here nine holes were created, a 2,800-yard layout that some called the most beautiful in the state.

The Dawson Golf Club was just pastureland at first, and so rocky that the greens were made of sand. Once a year sand was scraped from the Vermejo River, baked in blocks, mixed with oil, and then spread across the putting surfaces. The *Dawson News* reported in 1928, "The golf course is in excellent condition . . . there are no weeds on the fairway." What the paper failed to mention, however, were the presence of the occasional rattlesnake and stray cow.

Dues for the Dawson Golf Club initially were $12 a year. A Dawsonite could cover that by doing labor on the grounds, and many did. At its peak, the DGC had about sixty members. Few women played golf, and most miners felt they got enough exercise on the job. The club had no pro, but it did have a clubhouse, a shed that P.D. furnished from pieces of scrap.

Par at the Dawson Golf Club was thirty-six, and to say the course was demanding would be an understatement. Steep arroyos and rocky hillsides lay everywhere. Still, a lot of good golfers came out of Dawson, including Guy Moore, the sales manager in the main office; Pat Tiller, the undertaker; Doc Welch, the postmaster; railroader Agie Carlini; and Lawrence Brozovich, who, as a teenager, went to Albuquerque to play in the state high school tournament. One Dawsonite, Pete Marich, even went on to become a golf pro in California. Surely the most passionate golfer was Celso Chávez, the chief mine clerk. Chávez had learned the game as a Dawson kid. As an adult, he retired the club's coveted William D. Brennan Challenge Cup.

P. G. Flood's successor at Dawson was Leroy Brannon, another winner. Serving under Flood, Brannon had learned that, even if you had a good record, you hadn't accomplished anything unless you'd beat Raton. The Tigers showed up at the 1945 district basketball championships with an awesome

team, led by a six-foot-eight-inch redwood named Bill Gossett, later a professional player in Denver. Before the game, the Raton coach told Brannon, "We'll take it easy on you guys." That was all Brannon and his Miners needed to hear to get fired up. When little Chuy Ponce, about five foot six on a good day, went out for the opening jump against Gossett, the spectators howled. But when Ponce somehow got the ball, and fed it to Steve Schulte, who scored, jeers turned to cheers, more so after Dawson won, 23-20. Schulte, who had grown up dreaming of being a Miner, says, "Dawson never had much size, but we always had a lot of heart."

All the heart and fortitude in the world weren't enough to stop the exodus of people from Dawson during the 1940s. And those who stayed found that times were indeed changing. With a black student on the high school's basketball team, the Miners went to Clovis in the mid-1940s to play. When a restaurant there refused to serve the player, the rest of the team walked out. Reportedly, a similar event occurred in Carlsbad.

By this time Dawson had a schoolbus, an ancient, broken-down green thing with wooden sides. The driver, Max Dickman, kept the bus in Colfax and drove teams to games in it, once all the way to the Albuquerque Indian School, where the Miners watched Pueblo Indian dances at halftime. But the decrease in students negatively affected athletics in the town. The 1947 football team was a spotty 4-4-1. With the population plummeting, there were no more "rinky dinks," much less any substitutes. Cheerleaders still cheered, and the band still performed, though several members of the latter now were also football players: at halftime, clarinetist-halfback Jerry Scanlon simply marched across the field in his football uniform.

To be sure, some good athletes existed in this era, and

perhaps the finest was Jay Ragni. Along with his older brother Pete, Ragni had excelled in sports in high school, particularly in baseball. Like a lot of Dawsonites starting out in sports, Ragni had improvised: his first baseball had been made by his mother out of a ball of yarn. Ragni later became the batboy for Dawson's town team, and by age sixteen he was a lanky, left-handed pitcher and outfielder, playing with some men twice his age. "A natural," remembers Saracino. During World War II, Ragni was stationed with the navy in the San Francisco Bay area when he started playing baseball again. Soon a scout for the Oakland Oaks, a minor league Triple A team, spotted Ragni and signed him, making Ragni the only Dawsonite to ever play professional baseball. Jay Ragni spent seven years in the minor leagues, and gradually moved up through the ranks. One year he won nineteen games. Though he reached one rung below the major leagues, Ragni never quite made it to the big time.

The Miners of the 1940s managed to produce some gifted football players, such as Junior Pacheco, John Lancieri, and John Salvo, who later became a football coach at several New Mexico high schools. But Dawson struggled to make the statewide polls. Then, suddenly in 1948, the town—and the team—rallied beyond all expectations.

First, a new football field went up, northwest of the old ballpark. Named Fenlon Field, it honored the town's longtime superintendent. The old field, which Dawson had started using when Virgil Saracino was in grade school, was a rough, grassless patch of goatheads and cinders, a site as inhospitable as Dawson's crackerbox gym. And yet it was on that hardscrabble plain that Jay Ragni learned to field baseballs. "If you could catch a ground ball there," he says, "you could catch one anywhere."

Dawson's golf course attracted a loyal following, including, on this day, three visiting priests.

As a football field, the old ballpark left something to be desired: a ball kicked through the goalposts often got lost in the undergrowth. Fenlon Field had real grass. Phelps Dodge had furnished surveying and grading, and even supplied dynamite to uproot some mammoth cottonwoods. But the labor—the planting, tilling, rolling, watering, even the blasting—was done by townspeople.

Second, in its final years Dawson achieved the remarkable

by turning out some of its best football teams ever. There still were no divisions among New Mexico high schools at the time—big schools faced little schools—and Dawson, with one of the smallest student bodies in the state to play football, had an enrollment that yielded fewer than twenty players. Jerry Scanlon was a senior in the fall of 1948. A good student, musically adept and an Eagle Scout, Scanlon, at 140 pounds back then, considers playing football his greatest achievement in Dawson. "It was a way to be recognized in town; you became somebody." Scanlon's greatest moment in Dawson was playing a football game his senior year, a game that would decide the state championship.

That game took place November 20, 1948, and pitted Dawson against Tucumcari, in a battle of two unbeatens. Dawson, now coached by Ed Cleven, a former standout at Highlands University, had made an astonishing return to the polls that year, at one point climbing all the way to sixth place in the state. The game with Tucumcari would be a showdown. Five hundred and fifty fans from Tucumcari boarded a special Southern Pacific passenger train and rode the 132 miles to Dawson, arriving in time for the Saturday afternoon kickoff. More than 3,000 people, about twice Dawson's population at the time, crowded around Fenlon Field. Six area high school bands marched across the new grass. Radio play-by-play was sent back to Tucumcari over KTNM. Unfortunately for Dawson, Tucumcari came from behind to win, 13-6.

Dawson's final year of football was, in a way, even better. The Miners won their first seven games, crushing teams like Springer, 68-0. But then, on Thanksgiving Day, at Raton, with star quarterback Chubby Pacheco injured, the Miners fell, perhaps fittingly, to their oldest rival. The score was a heart-sickening 7-0. As if trying to prove something, Dawson had scored 223 points that farewell season. Its opponents had managed only 14.

The basketball team those last couple of years was equally impressive. In 1949, the Miners won twenty-one games and lost only two, by a total of three points. In the winter of 1950, only a month before the town was closed, for the second season in a row Dawson went to state, losing there to Tucumcari. Both years Dawson toppled powerhouse Albuquerque High.

Virgil Saracino watched all those games, even the final ones, as any loyal Dawsonite would. When Saracino left the town in 1950, he worked in steel mills and as a machinist. Today, he lives in Cokedale, Colorado, west of Trinidad, where every day he rides one of the three horses he owns, which helps explain why he is in such good shape, almost fit enough to still play for P. G. Flood.

After he finished at Dawson High, Saracino was offered a football scholarship by Denver University, but everything went wrong. "When I got up there, the job I was supposed to have wasn't open. So they stuck me in a fraternity house with those rich boys who dressed in suits, and I couldn't take it. Then they postponed freshman football. I got discouraged and caught a bus and came back to Dawson. I was from a small hick town, and I just flubbed it up. I had wanted to be a coach, but that never worked out."

Back in Dawson, Saracino took the controls of a steam shovel and was still working it, and still competing, when the town disappeared. "I was crazy about sports," he says. "Always have been. People ask me why; I'll tell you why. In Dawson, you kind of learned that, if things were going bad, sports could make 'em better."

Chapter Eight

FIGHTING

*"The feeling in town was that
what was worth living for
was worth fighting for."*

—Bob Lucero

There exists a number of people from Dawson who trace the serious repercussions of World War II to the day Louie Vitale was drafted.

Louie and his wife, Dorothy, owned Vitale's Barber Shop, three chairs and a beauty parlor in the back, run by Dorothy. With *Police Gazettes* on a corner table and the air heavy with witch hazel, Louie's shop, which stood on Main Street, next door to Central School, was a warm and inviting meeting hall, a place where a person could spend a pleasant hour getting a trim for fifty cents and stewing about the hated Raton Tigers.

The Vitales had been born and reared in Dawson, had studied tonsorial care in Chicago, and had come back to set up the business, which, since the mid-1930s, had grown into something of an institution. Louie had tooted clarinet in the Dawson High School band, had a beautiful tenor voice, and was a short, gregarious man who enjoyed talking to everyone. Same with Dorothy, who, it was generally agreed, delivered a dandy wash and set. The shop became a focal point, and then suddenly Louie was gone into the army and the place closed.

Oh, for a while Dorothy cut some people's hair over at her folks' house, but it just wasn't the same—for Dorothy or for Dawson. And certainly nobody was crazy about driving all the way to Raton to get a little taken off the top, for who really wanted to take a dig at the Raton Tigers on their home turf?

Louie Vitale's Barber Shop: a bellwether for World War II.

So, when Louie shut the door of his shop, it signaled loudly the hardships and reality of World War II.

The war, of course, did more than take away Louie's scissors. Other than the closing of the town in 1950, or one of the principal mine disasters, surely no single event had a greater impact on Dawson. The Great Depression eroded the town; the war scraped it clean. By 1944, 6 percent of Dawson's population had been drafted. An equal percentage had enlisted.

World War I had been felt: two Dawsonites lost their lives in that conflict, including one young man named Arthur Flynn, who had finally gotten the army to take him after being rejected several times for physical defects. In commemoration of that war, the Dawson-Springer football game was played for years on Armistice Day, and, following the 1923 mine explosion, all coffins of men who had served in the war were draped with the Stars and Stripes. Domenic Salvo, another Dawsonite who fought in World War I, had to wait until 1936 to receive any sort of honors, however. That was the

year when the United States government at last made good on long-overdue bonuses to veterans taken away from civilian jobs. Not long after he received his bonus, Salvo, a burly, red-haired miner, was seen proudly cruising Main Street in a spanking-new Ford. But the bulk of Dawson's population—particularly young men eligible for military service—didn't arrive until the 1920s, after World War I had ended. At the time of World War I, many of Dawson's fighting-age men were not even United States citizens.

By contrast, World War II had a major effect on Dawson—it removed numerous young males from the town, many of them permanently. To replace them, Phelps Dodge signed up older men to mine, and legend has it that P.D. was willing to hire "any sheepherder" who wandered into town. Many of the wartime recruits were inexperienced, and it's a wonder there weren't more major accidents, such as the one that killed Louis Trani in 1945. Trani, thirty-one, was putting up rail posts for high-tension lines when he was electrocuted, burned so badly the tacks on his shoes melted. Ralph Trani blamed a rookie supervisor, but it didn't bring back his dead son. Long a notable figure in town, a member of the elite coroner's jury that had investigated the 1923 mine explosion, the elder Trani was so heartbroken he sold his landmark boardinghouse and saloon, and moved to Colorado.

Still, even with the new work force—in 1942 mine employees numbered 377, the highest total since 1931—the war dictated a noticeable decline in Dawson residents, a slump that continued steadily until the last days, in 1950. By the end of 1941, Dawson's population was down to 2,000. The reduction was seen most in the outlying camps—Number Seven, Four Hill, Five Hill. Those who did stay moved toward downtown, altering Dawson's demographics. Another erosion of the town occurred in 1943 when John O'Brien, the first and only manager of the company ranch, died, and soon after the once prosperous place closed.

Eventually the war's presence was felt by Dawsonites in many ways and in places other than Vitale's darkened barbershop. When a resident picked up the *Raton Daily Range,* he found the war even on the comics page. In between boxing matches, the hero of "Joe Palooka" somehow found time to parachute behind enemy lines. When a Dawsonite went to the Phelps Dodge Mercantile, for fifteen cents he bought a pack of Camels because those cigarettes were "First in the Service," the favored smoke of men in the army, the navy, the marines, and the Coast Guard, "based on actual sales records in post exchanges and canteens." When he moseyed over to the Opera House and paid his dime, it might be to see Noel Coward's *In Which We Serve,* the movie for "all wartime sweethearts." On Wednesday nights, the Dawsonite tuned his Emerson radio, the one with knobs the size of walnuts, to KOB, catching the signal from Albuquerque and hearing the Fred Waring Orchestra play "Victory Tunes," brought to listeners by Chesterfield cigarettes. And if he stopped in after work at the Snake saloon, more than likely he would enter into a beery discussion of the German *Blitzkrieg,* which, if truth be known, was only slightly more despised than the Raton Tigers.

The war also affected coal production. There was a concerted effort in town to produce more coal for the American fighting machine, and consequently the one mine now working in town, Number Six, stayed open seven days a week. Coal production increased from 234,000 tons in 1940 to 374,000 tons in 1944. But those figures are misleading, for the mines' highest wartime production of coal equaled only 55 percent of the town's average yearly production from 1902 to 1950.

How to explain the slowdown? Fewer men were employed, for one thing. During the first five years of the Great Depression, Dawson averaged 365 employees. By the end of the war, that figure had dropped to 300. Coal strikes hurt output, too. A nationwide strike that lasted sixty-seven days in 1943 damaged Dawson financially and emotionally, though life went on. Dawson news notes in the *Raton Daily Range* dutifully reported a piano recital by Margaret Kuper's students, the regular Wednesday afternoon meeting of the Extension Club, and even Henry Munz's tonsilectomy.

Many in town who went on strike during the height of the war did so reluctantly, since some of these miners had sons in uniform, sons fighting in the European Theatre, fighting from Anzio to Zagreb, in the old country. To walk out during wartime was like turning against one's new country. And yet, the government of the new country could act irrationally. On a few occasions during the war the FBI showed up in Dawson to confiscate weapons from Italian immigrants. Like Japanese-Americans in California, in wartime Italians were somehow considered threatening. Miner Joe Minelli had a shotgun and shortwave radio removed from his house. From Clemente Di Domenico, a tippleman, the government took a sixteen-gauge shotgun. Incredibly, both Dawson men had sons serving in the United States Army.

Despite this shameful treatment, just about everyone in Dawson was overwhelmingly patriotic—and it showed. Atop Scout Hill, in the center of town, the huge American flag, estimated to be thirty feet by fifty feet, seemed to fly more regularly during the war. Down at the Mercantile, in a spot seen by all, an honor board noted Dawson men and women serving their country. And up the street at the Catholic church, another placard, this one by the altar, listed men who had lost their lives. In backyards and in side yards, in vacant lots and by the irrigation ditch, Dawsonites tended victory gardens. Wives, girlfriends, mothers, and volunteer members of the Dawson branch of the American Red Cross created between June 1941 and January 1944 the following: thirty-seven pairs of socks, fourteen turtleneck sweaters, six shirts, fifty-five refugee sweaters, fourteen army helmets, four large scarves, and sixty-five pairs of pajamas. A booth at the high school was set up to sell war bonds, and for $18.75 a student bought a stamp-filled booklet that could be redeemed for a $25.00 bond and a lot of civic pride. Even little kids in Dawson did their part for the men and women "Over There." Jerry Scanlon was one of a bunch of youngsters who collected tinfoil, much of it from scraps off those "First in the Service" packs of Camel cigarettes. The tinfoil was packed into big balls. Gather enough tinfoil, the belief went, and you could build an airplane.

The war appeared to bond even tighter the ethnically diverse Dawson residents, and thus fuse those backgrounds into one common homeland. Indeed, Dawson's enlistees represented every nationality and every branch. Henry English, an electrician, chose the navy; for Pete Córdova, a pick miner, it was the marines; Michael Gustovich, a scraperman, went into the army; and machine operator Fred Marcelli joined the Coast Guard.

And yet as much spirit as Dawsonites had for their country, going off to war never was an easy task. Alberta McClary saw her husband cry for the first time when their son, Bob, enlisted in the navy. Electrician Terence Scanlon watched, presumably with mixed emotions, as four of his sons left home for the war. There was no such thing as a "conscientious objector" in Dawson. Even older men such as Celso Chávez, who was in his mid-thirties and had a family when the war got going, felt peculiar about not being in uniform.

Phelps Dodge was generous to those employees who departed for the service. The company gave each man a month's wages when he entered the military and the promise of a job within ninety days after he got back. There were, however, occasional mix-ups. When Kelly Mora came back to town, he was told there were no mine jobs: "Mr. Arnold was the manager then, and I told him, 'Look, while I was on the battlefield getting shot at, you were sitting with your fat rear end on the desk here.' Then I walked out of the office. He called and said, 'Look, Kelly, come back here.' So I got back in the mines."

The 52-20 Club, a governmental welfare fund, helped many returning GIs. Veterans would go down to the main office in Dawson once a week to check on job offerings. If there wasn't any work available in a field he wanted, the veteran was given $20. Roger Scanlon, fresh out of the navy, stopped in at the office every Monday and asked, with tongue firmly planted in cheek, if they had any listings for bank president. Scanlon, of course, knew no bank president jobs existed, because no bank existed in Dawson. But he had no intention of going into the mines. Nonetheless, Scanlon would be given his $20, which he took straight to the Snake. "There was about twenty or thirty of us boys did that, and my $20 would last about a couple of weeks. I'd stay there and play cards from about 10:00 A.M. to midnight." Scanlon belonged to Dawson's 52-20 Club for about a year, or the limit. "It was great fun. After a while I got a job at the Mercantile. I was an iceman. I sold ice off a truck around town. Those blocks weighed about twenty-five pounds each, and I hated it. In 1948, I decided to rejoin the navy."

Dawson resembled a lot of towns during the war in that

there were occasional blackout drills, and every once in a while P-38s, from Crews Field near Raton, would roar over the canyons around the town. And, like most Americans, Dawsonites learned to scrimp. Gasoline ration books were common sights; for the first time since the 1920s, nobody motored off to Trinidad or Clayton or even to Cimarron just for the heck of it on a Sunday afternoon. For some canned goods and meats, red and blue stamps were in evidence, but the only items in terribly short supply were silk stockings and sugar. And yet certain foods, especially meat and dairy products originating from the company ranch, were reasonably plentiful. No one, however, had much money.

The mines weren't the only place to experience problems due to Dawson's dwindling wartime population. Up at the high school, most classes had a far greater number of girls than boys. In fact, during 1943 and 1944 Dawson High did not have a football team—there were simply not enough players to make one. In 1943, eight young men, all seniors, enlisted before the school year ended. When it came time for graduation, their parents stepped forward and received their sons' diplomas. Girls picked up their own diplomas, of course, and they did so proudly; it was the first year graduates wore commencement gowns, front-page news in the *Raton Daily Range.*

Life for Dawson women during the war was often lonely, so letters from overseas were greatly appreciated. Goldie Whiteley so enjoyed her son Bill's letters from England that she gave them to the Raton paper to reproduce on the front page, as did the parents of Emilio Ghiglieri, who was serving in Europe. "Belgium," wrote Sgt. Ghiglieri, "has a lot of coal mines, and it reminds me of home; but they are not up to date as the mines in the states."

The post office, located in the old bank building, was a

Although the war decimated the high school's enrollment, the 1943 Miners still took third place in the state basketball tournament.

Nick Di Domenico joined his sisters and brother in Dawson during a 1941 furlough.

popular gathering spot in Dawson during the war. After postmaster Doc Welch wakened from one of his periodic naps, he would, for three cents, sell you a first-class stamp. Receiving mail was, for many in Dawson, a high point of the day. For Isabel Viramontes, a letter from her husband, Chon, serving in Italy, was almost like speaking to him. "Chon used to send me poems in the mail when he was in the army. Sometimes the mail would be delayed, and then suddenly I'd get two or three letters at a time. I could always tell when I got a letter from Chon. Mr. Bessolo [Frank Bessolo, Dawson's longtime rural mail carrier] would honk his horn on the way up Capitan—just for me."

With such a small male population in Dawson, single women in town found dates hard to come by. Thus, when an unattached serviceman returned home, he quickly became one of the chief attractions in the community. In 1945, when Nick

Di Domenico waltzed back into town from his army post in Texas, he was a buck sergeant looking for a good time. The first order of business was to drop in at the Sweet Shop and figure out where to go and with whom. All the time young people in town were putting nickels in the Sweet Shop's big Wurlitzer jukebox to hear "Boogie Woogie Bugle Boy." But what they really wanted to hear—*and dance to*—was a live band. So one night, while Nick was on furlough and tapping his foot in the Sweet Shop, he got paired with Margie Bergamo. The couple had known each other in high school. Heck, they'd known each other since kindergarten. But no sparks had ever flown. Margie, in fact, had for several years maintained a strong dislike for Nick. That night, however, Nick and Margie and some others, in search of a live band, wound up in Springer at the 85 Club. Sometime during the evening, Margie took a good look at Nick, studied him in his uniform, with his newly attached chevrons and his big service cap shoved back at a jaunty angle. All of a sudden she saw him in a different light. By the time Nick got back to Texas, he found two letters from Margie waiting for him. The couple were married in 1948.

GIs returning to Dawson on leave were given an enthusiastic welcome. Frequently a furloughed GI would head up the hill for the high school, where he would often be called upon by the principal, Marion Douds, to give a speech in his uniform. Douds helped the war effort—and gained fans among Dawson's young men—by personally writing letters to many of her ex-students who were in the military. When a young Hispanic serviceman came home on leave, his family often held a *baile,* or small fiesta, in his honor. There would be Mexican music, and the serviceman would stand there, in uniform, and tell what it was like in the war. Joe Andazola returned home from action in Italy to find his wife, Josephine, waiting for him at the train station in Raton with the infant son he had never seen.

For Dawson's young men—and a handful of women, such as Sylvia Peppin, who served in the WAVES—the war proved to be an education. "Before the war," says Anna Lucero, "most Slavs in Dawson married Slavs. Italians married Italians, Greeks married Greeks. The war changed all that. As close as Dawson was, people started marrying beyond their nationalities." Indeed, being in the service showed many young Dawsonites that a world existed beyond the town's borders. The exodus of Dawson's youth had begun in the Great Depression, but the war seemed to drive home the point that "once a miner, always a miner," simply didn't have to be true. The war broadened horizons and helped young men and women understand that there were other opportunities to be explored and other people to meet. Ultimately then, the war was in part responsible for Dawson's demise.

The education that Dawson's servicemen received frequently was unexpected. Perfecto "Chubby" Pacheco knew little about prejudice until he entered the military. "Growing up in Dawson," says Pacheco, "there was no telling what your neighbor's nationality was. As a kid, my friends were Johnny Lancieri, an Italian; John Starkovich, a Slavic; and Jerry Scanlon, an Irishman. They came to my house, and I went to theirs. I ate out of their iceboxes, and they ate out of mine. I didn't see any differences between them. But when I got to the army, there were three Mexicans in my whole company. Rank didn't come easy to us, and I felt the discrimination. I felt bypassed."

Conversely, Gabe Trujillo says that coming from Dawson helped him during the war. "My experiences in the service showed me that people who were exposed to only one cultural group growing up had all sorts of trouble adjusting and being away from home. I didn't have those problems. I had grown up with a Pascetti, a Gonzáles, a Brozovich, a Hancock, and Manuel Katsufrakis, a Greek, who later went on to become a distinguished judge in California. When I was living in Dawson in the 1930s, life was quite primitive by today's standards. We had no inside toilets, no cars, and we ran everywhere. In basic training in the army, you lived in some pretty bad barracks, so all that helped. And we ran everywhere, so I was used to that."

Like most Americans during the war, Dawsonites dreaded the appearance of the Western Union man coming up the street. In fact, Flora and Henry Peppin, who had three sons in uniform, used to rush back inside their house and busy themselves whenever they spotted the telegram messenger, hoping by doing something else they could somehow make

Cadet Bill Whiteley was one of a number of young men and women who left Dawson and, for the first time, saw another part of the world.

him pass by their home. Usually this worked. And then, of course, one day the Western Union man did stop at the Peppins, just a couple of blocks up from the Mercantile. While their daughter, Sylvia, looked on with eyes wide as oysters, the couple tore at the envelope with nervous fingers, all the while wondering which son they would never see again. It was George, the telegram said, their middle son, a member of the 45th Infantry Division. But George only had been wounded, thank God.

Other young men weren't so lucky. Because Dawson's families were so close-knit, a serviceman's death almost always had a profound effect on the entire community. Mike Carlini had been a high school football star in the 1930s. Months after

he died in the Battle of the Bulge, dozens of Dawsonites were still visiting his grave in Mount Calvary Cemetery in Raton. Emery King, another accomplished football player, was buried in the Philippines, after being killed in action on Mindanao. Dawsonites were stunned: King had only been in the service six months. Vincent Vandersarl had been a well-liked kid in prewar Dawson High—smart, athletic, musical, and one of the first teenagers in town to own a car, a convertible coupe. Of course, it helped that Vincent's father was a mechanic and ran the only garage in Dawson. Vincent lived in a house behind Gene Scanlon, and the two played baseball together, double-dated, and became inseparable. During the war, Scanlon, in the navy, wrote regularly to Vandersarl, a pilot in the Army Air Corps. While stationed in the Admiralty Islands in the South Pacific, Scanlon received a letter one day that he'd already sent to his boyhood friend. It had "DECEASED" stamped on the outside of the envelope. "I wrote my dad in Dawson and asked what was going on," says Scanlon. "He wrote back saying that Vincent's plane had been lost on a flight from India to Burma, over what they called 'The Hump.' They never found any sign of that plane. And Vincent's mother never really believed he died. Me, I sometimes still can't believe Vincent's gone."

Two war stories illustrate how having roots in Dawson could be a powerful influence on someone's life.

Mary Frances García Reza: "I was a little girl and was living with my grandmother, Frances B. Lopez, during the war. Like a lot of Hispanic families in Dawson, my grandmother raised me, even though my mother lived right next door. My grandmother was a wonderful, devout woman who baked for everybody. One morning, a young stranger came down out of the mountains north of town. He was tall and blond and handsome; but he seemed lost and tired. We had had news the past few days in Dawson that two German prisoners had escaped from this camp they had at Trinidad. If my grandmother thought this was an escaped prisoner, she didn't let on. She just saw him standing on her step. In the few English words she knew, she said, 'Come, come.' And he came in.

"My grandmother gave him a ladle and water, and he drank and drank and drank. Then she gave him some homemade bread, and he ate and ate and ate. He sat there in the kitchen drinking and eating, and my grandmother just kept bringing the food and didn't ask any questions. I was so young, I just stood there watching.

"In the middle of all this, my mother telephoned. She worked at the Phelps Dodge office, and she said to my grandmother, 'Now be careful, don't let anyone in the house.' My grandmother, of course, totally ignored the call. Finally, the young man was filled up and rested, and he got up to go. My grandmother said, 'May God go with you.'

"Later that night, at supper, everybody was sitting around talking about these escaped prisoners. My grandmother didn't say a word. Finally, she mumbled, 'I pray that they don't find him.' I don't know what happened next, but I guess I somehow let out that my grandmother had fed this young man. Everybody at the table was suddenly upset, and then my grandmother said, 'My two sons are overseas in the war. May they treat Eddie and Julio as I have treated this young man.'

"Sometime later they found both of the escaped prisoners and sent them back to Trinidad. I've always wondered—did our young man remember my grandmother? Did he remember Dawson?"

Bob Lucero: "Three years, six months, one day and three hours. That's how long I was in prison in the Philippines. I

Incarcerated in a Japanese prison camp,
Bob Lucero hung onto Dawson memories.

was part of that Bataan Death March, the one that killed nearly 10,000 servicemen. Yeah, I've got to say that Dawson played a role in helping me survive.

"I was drafted in March of '41 and captured by the Japanese in April of '42, in Mariveles, in the Philippines. The Japs captured this hospital where I was. I'd gone there after a Jeep accident, thinking I'd broken my ankle.

"We started marching to our prison, Cabanatuan, Camp Number One, fifty-some miles away. A lot of the men, of course, died along the way, of starvation and lack of water. It was 110 in the shade, and there wasn't any shade.

"When we got to the prison camp, it was no better. Dysentery, malaria, malnutrition—they were all a big part of it. Men were dying all the time. In Cabanatuan, I ran into three other Dawsonites—Johnny Blazovich, Freddie Archuleta, and Delbert Covert. Small world. All three of them died right there in the camp. I was assigned to the burial detail, and one day when I picked up this man, he seemed familiar. It was Johnny.

"What kept me alive? I made it through because I was taken care of by a group of nine or ten guys. We stuck together. When I had malaria, they stood me up and forced me to eat; they held my mouth open and stuffed raw rice down me. Being from Dawson helped me to make it, I know. See, I didn't mistrust anybody. In Dawson, there was no such thing as a lock and key. If you were a loner and didn't pitch in or were suspicious of someone in Cabanatuan, you had less of a chance to make it. You needed friends there. Good friends. I could have escaped a hundred times, but the Japs had this 'blood brothers' thing. If one guy escaped, they'd pick out ten others and shoot them in front of you. I saw enough of that to convince me that life was pretty cheap over there.

"My biggest hope was that I'd be able to see my family again in Dawson. I hung on to that. When we were finally liberated in Manila, I got a troop ship home. Most of the fellas on the ship had been through Bataan, and we looked a sight. One day I saw this guy who seemed familiar. It was Ed Dahl, and I'd worked in the mines with him. He'd been in the Seabees. He didn't recognize me, probably because I went into the army weighing 170 pounds and came out weighing about 90 pounds.

"Back in the states, I went to Bruns Army Hospital in Santa Fe. They had to get us fattened up. Just before Thanksgiving I got a train from Lamy to Raton, where my brother Dave picked me up. I came into Dawson at night, and I guess it was a surprise. Dad and Mother knew I was alive, but they weren't expecting me. There was a lot of crying and hugging, and it was good to be home. I'd been away from Dawson for four years, and that was much too long."

When word reached Dawson in September of 1945 that the Japanese had surrendered, Bill Hancock, his sister Jessie, and his mother Nellie climbed into the Hancocks' 1937 Chevy and, followed by other cars, drove up and down the town's little streets, honking their horn. Over at the power plant, Scottie Covert blew the whistle, but, for the first time ever, it sounded in celebration, not to alert residents of an accident. Down at the Snake, barkeep Herb Mitchell announced that beer was on the house.

People in Dawson truly knew the war was over when Louie Vitale came home from the Pacific and reopened his barbershop. Louie had some bad news, however—a haircut would now cost seventy-five cents.

Chapter Nine

ENDING

"People were crying in the street."
—Amelia Lopez García

Jeanette O'Belmito stood behind the butcher's counter at the Phelps Dodge Mercantile that Saturday afternoon and wondered what all the fuss was about. Everybody had gone to Raton for a basketball game, so Dawson should have been quiet. But there was definitely something in the air. Suddenly, someone came by the meat department and, all out of breath, asked Jeanette, "Didja hear the news?"

"What news?" said Jeanette, as she sliced some bologna.

"They're closing the town!"

For a second, Jeanette thought her heart might stop. *Closing the town!* The town was all she knew; it was her whole life. She'd been born in Dawson in the winter of 1914, up at Loreta in a house so drafty that Jeanette's mother, Frances, had put her crib on the floor because snow was coming through the windows. Jeanette's father, John, was a miner. Not long after landing in this country from Italy, John O'Belmito had his name changed for him—by an Irish immigration officer. John and Frances O'Belmito reared seven kids in that drafty, little house at Loreta, and taught them all to work hard. Jeanette, in fact, who only reached the sixth grade in Dawson, quit school to go to work. She put in more than twelve years at the town hospital, changing bedpans, scrubbing walls, doing all the jobs no one else would do. Then she hired on at the Phelps Dodge Mercantile. And now, on February 25, 1950, as she stood in the company store, Jeanette worried about the future. Her father was dead and the other kids gone, so it was just Jeanette and her mother, alone in a house downtown with a nice garden. As she wrapped luncheon meats, Jeanette couldn't help but wonder what would happen to the two of them. Everything they needed was right here in Dawson; why, they didn't even own a car. Mr. Beall, who ran the company store, had been so good to Jeanette. In fact, everything seemed almost perfect, until that Saturday afternoon when she heard the news.

Many townspeople heard about the closing in a manner that only later seemed appropriate—while following a sports event. On Friday February 24, 1950, Dawson beat Clayton, and coach P. G. Flood, in the District One basketball semifinals at Raton. On Saturday afternoon, before the district finals, the *Raton Range* appeared with a jolting front-page story. A letter from Stag Cañon Branch manager G. O. Arnold to John L. Lewis, president of the United Mine Workers of America, announced the end of the town. ''We herewith give you notice of our plan to close down the Dawson mine on or before April 30, 1950,'' wrote Arnold. ''Effective April 30, 1950, we hereby cancel all obligations and agreements, either expressed or implied, which may be part of any wage agreement with your union.'' Arnold added that none of the Dawson people would be transferred to other jobs.

Shock waves spread across Raton, where scores of Dawsonites, though not Jeanette O'Belmito, had gathered to watch the district finals. The timing of the news was especially bad, people agreed: Dawson miners, along with more than 350,000 others across the country, had been on strike since mid-January. Wives had already stretched food budgets to the breaking point, and many children had only one set of clothes with more patches than a pirate ship. *How could anybody afford this?* When copies of the *Raton Range* made their way into the Silver Dollar, a great sadness fell over the Raton bar. That night, a copy of the article was posted near the entrance to the Raton High School gym, in case someone still hadn't heard, which seemed doubtful.

As a town, Dawson had stared adversity in the face often. Hence, it was not about to go out with a whimper. Instead, the boys' basketball team, meeting the only unbeaten high school squad in the state, played the game of their lives. With two minutes to go and holding a one point lead, the Roy Longhorns tried to freeze the ball. Dawson, applying a desperation defense, forced Roy to bobble a pass with forty-five seconds left. Lee Martínez then sank a free throw to tie the game. Dawson got the ball back again, and Martínez was fouled once more. With ten seconds left, he stepped to the line and coolly made both free throws. The Miners had beaten Roy High School 36-34 to become District One champions.

Bedlam filled the gym, which earlier in the evening had resembled a morgue. For Dawson fans, the victory represented one final moment to celebrate something positive. Said the *Raton Range* of the game: ''It couldn't have been any better if it had been rehearsed and put on by a Hollywood studio.''

The following day, however, the news of the town's closing began to sink in. For many, the announcement had been like a punch to the stomach, comparable in its unexpectedness to the death of Franklin D. Roosevelt five years earlier. Others said it was no surprise—that they'd known for years Dawson was dying and that it was just a matter of time.

After the initial tears dried, some townspeople, like mine superintendent Fritz Koelling, attempted to interest a corporation in taking over the town. Surely, Koelling reasoned, a manufacturer could set up a factory in the Mercantile, still a sturdy brick building. Another group of residents tried to lease Mine Number Six for a small-scale operation, and still others asked Phelps Dodge if they could live on in Dawson past June 30, when the town would be closed entirely. To all of these proposals, P.D. said no. P.D. did insist the school year be completed, however, and students would attend classes six days a week to make it. The high school's senior class—all twenty students—would graduate on time. Where would kids go to school the next year? No one knew, though some neighboring towns, interested in enlisting Dawson athletes for the local high school, reportedly offered to look for jobs for the young men's fathers.

Raton, once something of a rival for Dawsonites, now appeared as a city trying to gain their affection. In fact, Raton's mayor, Clarence Healey, welcomed Dawson refugees. Healey told the *Raton Range,* "All Raton sympathizes deeply with the people of Dawson in their tragedy." The Monday after the announcement of the closing, Hannah McGarvey, a pillar of Dawson's schools, was seen weeping in the hall of Central School. "Don't cry, Miss McGarvey," said a small boy. "You'll get a job. Everybody knows you." McGarvey eventually became principal of Kearney Elementary School—in Raton. Between the end of April 1950 and June of that year, it was estimated that 400 Dawsonites had settled in Raton.

When the nationwide coal strike finally ended March 6, Stag Cañon kept Number Six Mine open five days a week, so townspeople would have something saved when the end came. At the same time, however, Phelps Dodge cut off credit at the company store and made known that outstanding debts at the store would be deducted from the last paycheck.

June 30, a date that back in February had seemed a com-

SATURDAY, FEBRUARY 25, 1950 — Associated Press Leased Wire Service

Dawson Mine Closing April 30; Notice Posted By Company At Noon; 1,200 Persons At Camp

This Raton Range *article heralded the beginning of the end.*

The 1200 residents of Dawson were notified today of plans to close the Dawson mine April 30, 1950.

The notice came in the form of a copy of a letter from G. O. Arnold, manager of the Stag Canon branch of the Phelps Dodge corporation, to John L. Lewis, president of the United Mine Workers of America. A copy of the letter was posted on bulletin boards at Dawson at noon today.

The letter:

Mr. John L. Lewis, President
United Mine Workers of America
United Mine Workers' building
Washington 5, D. C.

Dear Sir:

We herewith give you notice of our plan to close down the Dawson mine on or before April 30, 1950. Effective April 30, 1950, we hereby cancel all obligations and agreements, either expressed or implied, which may be a part of any wage agreement with your union; this applies especially to the wage agreement made effective July 1, 1948, and presumably extended to cover present operations, and to any subsequent wage agreement which may become effective betwen now and April 30, 1950.

It is the intent to operate the Dawson mine until April 30, 1950, provided the action of your union makes such operation possible and economically advisable.

Yours very truly
(signed) G. O. Arnold,
Manager

fortable distance, now suddenly loomed closer than ever for Dawson's 1,250 residents. By early spring, pickup trucks, piled high with possessions, started to show up around town, and classified ads such as the following started appearing in the *Raton Range:*

> 4 rooms of furniture,
> including electric
> stove and refrigerator.

For many men, such as Jack Buttram, who had a wife and a young daughter and had lived in Dawson all his life, there was worry. "We'll find something," he told a *Denver Post* reporter, "but right now I don't have the slightest idea what it will be." Coal miners surely had the most to fear. A handful landed jobs in nearby Koehler, the only area coal mine still going. Other miners, such as Abe Trujillo and Margarito Martínez, had to go to Valdez, Colorado. Some even went to Utah. Miners close to age fifty had the hardest time. Their age worked against them, not only to get work, but to qualify for a pension. When Mine Number Six closed, it was estimated that only 25 percent of Dawson's 200 union members found jobs. County relief and unemployment helped here and there, and some of the younger miners went to college on the GI Bill, which they had been postponing. A few found jobs on area ranches or looked for any kind of work in Albuquerque. "Get another trade," Nick Gonzáles, secretary of the local, advised young miners. "Coal mining is shot, as far as northern New Mexico is concerned." The union, which had a small welfare fund, tried to assist, but there was little it could do, for the bylaws said nothing about a town closing.

The finality began to build, often in small, sad ways. On April 14, the ever-shrinking "Dawson News" column in the *Raton Range* contained this note: "Dawson entertained eleven little Brownies at the Robert Compton home, April 7, with a 'farewell' party for them all." A day later, the last junior-senior prom was held, music by Whited's Orchestra. On April 22, the contents of the high school's jam-packed trophy case were carted to the Colfax County Courthouse in Raton.

Stag Cañon officials decided that April 28, a Friday, would be the last day Number Six would operate, and, as that date approached, the anxiety increased. Ona Randall, who taught at Douglas School, remembers schoolchildren coming up to her those last few weeks with red-rimmed eyes. "They'd sob, 'We don't know any place but Dawson.' And, you know, some of them hadn't even been to Raton. So we cried with them."

At 1:30 P.M., April 28, 1950, the 138 miners still at work filled Dawson's last trip of ore cars. The final car reached the tipple at about 3:00 that afternoon, where Davis Yob, Joe Manelli, and others splashed it with beer. Finally, Fred Bergamo dumped the car, stopping just before he did to pose for a photograph. A few minutes later, Stach DiLorenzo, who had lost a hand to Number Six, hung up his helmet for the last time. A party—one reveler likened it to the "desperate gaity of a wake"—followed in the tipple shack. Even Gerald Arnold, the Stag Cañon Branch manager, dropped by. Dawson's closing truly saddened Arnold, despite his curt announcement in the newspaper. He lamented, "The silence will be deafening around here in a few weeks, I'm afraid."

A few hours later, across town at the Dawson Golf Club, thirty or so more men gathered in the clubhouse for hamburgers and beer. Mostly mine office employees and foremen, the group turned out to be a veritable Who's Who of Dawson, from Marshall Flint, the warehouse manager, to Crozier Hart, the veteran physician. Decorum mattered little: Nick Di

Domenico showed up from a softball game still wearing his Snake saloon team sweatshirt, and Ted Shelton, the town supervisor, took off his suit coat to put on an apron. Even Mac McClary, Stag Cañon Branch's dedicated chief clerk, loosened his necktie a bit. Celso Chávez, chief mine clerk, raised a can of beer in toast. 'This,'' said Chávez, bestowing a permanent name to the affair, ''is the Last Hurrah.''

At the Opera House that evening, coal miner-turned-musician Augustine Hernández, with guitar in hand, presented a program of Spanish songs he had written especially for the occasion. There were speeches that night, but they would soon be forgotten. Not Hernández's ballads, however. ''There wasn't a dry eye in the house,'' says Albert Rivera. From ''Adios a Dawson'':

> Farewell mountains of Dawson
> Farewell mines of coal
> I swear that even though I'm gone
> I'll carry you in my heart.

The following day, the town discontinued medical services, and by Sunday, April 30, vacant houses with curtainless windows could be seen across the community. Word of the exodus drew the curious. ''People would come up from Albuquerque and try to buy stuff and offer you nothing,'' grumps Verge Saracino. ''One guy wanted to buy my kitchen set. I told him I'd take an axe to it before I'd sell it to him.'' Some visitors didn't even bother to ask what was for sale. ''My wife, Patricia, and I went to Raton one day, and when we came back we found someone had gone in our house and stolen furniture,'' says Margarito Martínez. For the first time ever, Dawsonites began to lock their doors. The mammoth Phelps Dodge Mercantile had a particular appeal to out-of-town scavengers. ''If they couldn't buy anything, they would take it,'' says Jeanette

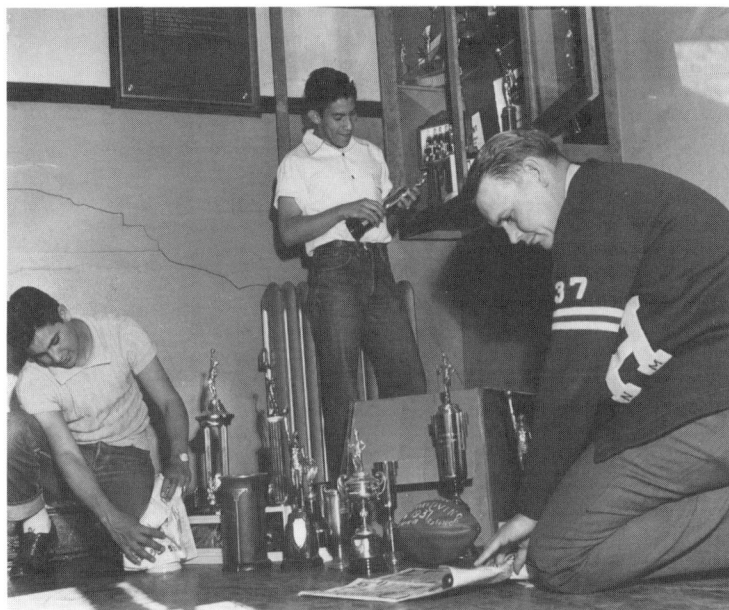

Packing up school memorabilia meant getting one step closer to abandonment.

O'Belmito. ''They were ripping out cherry wood counters from the store. It really upset me, but I didn't have enough sense to stop them.''

A state labor official arrived May 1 to take unemployment claims. Meanwhile, Stag Cañon's payroll department hurried to prepare the final checks by May 6. The moment Mine Number Six was closed and sealed, as the other nine mines in town had been earlier, P.D. removed Dawson from the tax rolls of Colfax County, creating an economic shortfall of nearly $2 million. Shortly, the county would lose 18 percent of its population and 32 percent of its economy. On May 5, the last issue of the *Miner's Pick*, Dawson High School's student newspaper, appeared. "Let the dead bury their dead," wrote editor Mary Alice Ybarra. "I love Dawson for what it has meant to me and the thousands of other people who have lived here. And if Dawson is to become a memory, then thank God it is a beautiful memory." Four days later, Celso Chávez drove Jeanette O'Belmito and her mother to Raton. "We didn't know where to go," says Jeanette. "We didn't have any place in mind at all." Eventually, the two women took a train to California.

On May 11, commencement was held in the Opera House for Dawson High School's last graduating class. It was a bittersweet evening for senior Fred Cericola. He had edited the last copy of the *Miner's Lamp,* the school yearbook, played basketball and football for Dawson's last teams, and had played baritone in Dawson's last marching band. Now he was the school's last valedictorian. Onstage, as Cericola looked out and saw his mother smiling proudly, he couldn't help but think of his father, who had been the last man killed in a Dawson mine, only nine months before. In his valedictory speech, Cericola tried to strike a positive note for young Dawsonites who had always expected to go into the mines after graduation. "Now we have the opportunity to do something else," Cericola said.

As the end drew nearer, sorrowful sights became commonplace. Celso Chávez could be seen standing in the middle of Main Street burning office records in two huge incinerators. Townspeople who got behind in their rent suddenly found their power and lights turned off, something that would never have happened before. On May 15, an official from Phelps Dodge headquarters in Douglas, Arizona, arrived to make final arrangements for what the company termed "the greatest sale in the history of the Southwest." The first step in that sale came on June 6, when P.D. sold to the National Iron and Metal Company of Phoenix all the aboveground property in the town for $500,000. Within a few days, National Iron began salvaging most of the structures and machinery for scrap, and selling everything else, from hospital beds to pencil sharpeners.

Salvage officials moved into the Stag Cañon Branch office and retained about fifty men. Those workers who had families would stay in the dozen or so houses left standing in Number Seven Camp or downtown. One of the first buildings wrecked was St. John the Baptist Catholic Church. Though the church was stone and couldn't be moved, its swift razing struck a nerve. Years before, town Catholics had asked Phelps Dodge for a deed to the church. The company had said no and thus had leased it from the beginning. There was some solace: St. John's pews went to a church in Albuquerque's South Valley, and its organ went to Española. No one wanted to see the Opera House go down either, and it stood until after a county primary election was held in the building's polling room, on June 6. Some of the Opera House's interior was saved, too: the projection and sound equipment, draperies, and stage settings went to the Mesa Theater in Roy. On June 13, Roush and Guest, an Albuquerque house-moving company, purchased 400 Dawson residences from National Iron and Metal Company. The old coke breeze block houses would be torn down, but the wooden ones were put on sale and Dawsonites, aware of a housing shortage in the area, quickly snapped them up. Most of the dwellings went to northeastern New Mexico, to Clayton and Raton in particular. Some, however, were trucked as far away as Oklahoma and Texas. Left untouched would be only the non-company buildings in town, those owned by the Southern Pacific Railroad, the United States Post Office, and the Frontier Power Company of Trinidad, which ran the

*Some Dawsonites moved what belongings they could,
including, on occasion, the house itself.*

big plant that sat near the center of Dawson and supplied power to northeastern New Mexico and southern Colorado.

As June 30 approached, the scene became almost unbearable. Ted Shelton, who had been born in a tent in Dawson, before houses even were built, and had grown up to take a responsible position in the community, watched forlornly as men demolished it. Sighing, Shelton said, ''There never was a town like this before, and there never will be again.''

Yet, for some Dawsonites, the end served as motivation. ''I think it did people a favor when it closed,'' says Josephine Valdez Trujillo. ''People got out and got their own homes. When they lived in Dawson, what could they have? Nothing. Many families lived from day to day. When the town closed, it forced people to go out and find a job, buy a house, get an education. For the first time in their lives, they had to do something on their own.''

Celso Chávez pulled out July 4. He had been the last man on the company payroll, and he was quitting. Phelps Dodge had offered Chávez, as it did a few others, a job in Arizona. But Chávez moved to Santa Fe instead; he couldn't bear to get too far away from Dawson. Chávez, the son of a mule train driver, had lived in the town since 1917. ''It was really hard letting go,'' he says. ''We all knew it was going to close, but still . . . '' People still asked: how could anyone shut down a town that had a physical worth of $100 million? Or close mines that held at least 35 million tons of coal? How could anyone stand by and let die a community that once was home to nearly 6,000 people?

In truth, Dawson began to die almost as soon as it reached its glory, and there had been signs of a terminal illness as early as World War I. When the war caused the country's coal needs to be curtailed, three mines in Dawson closed. By 1919,

the labor force in Dawson had dropped from 1,378 to 1,005. Because the town had acquired a weekly newspaper and a new high school in the 1920s, prosperity seemed again on the horizon. But in actuality Dawson was headed toward an early grave. The demand for bituminous coal in 1921 skidded to a low that hadn't been seen since 1906. Simply, the industry found itself with too much. Rising competition from other fuels, such as oil, gas, and hydroelectricity, further threatened the coal industry.

Coke presented a similarly alarming problem for Dawson. Stag Cañon had produced 304,000 tons of coke in 1917, but four years later that figure had fallen to 32,000. Setbacks in the copper industry, which depended on coke, could be seen most vividly at the opposite corner of New Mexico, in the copper mining town of Tyrone, near Silver City. Phelps Dodge had acquired Tyrone in 1909 and had poured a great deal of money into it, more even than into Dawson. Tyrone, in fact, became known as the most beautiful and modern mining town in the United States. But the erosion of nationwide copper prices caused the town to fold in 1921.

Though the 1923 explosion drew Dawsonites closer, no amount of esprit de corps or new facilities could stop the town's economic slide. Many residents were not aware of the situation, or at least chose to ignore it. Instead, they buoyed their faith in the future on the town's new swimming pool or the newly installed tennis courts. Some townspeople, of course, recognized the signs of weakness clearly. Optimism, however, rose in 1924 when the stalwart Southern Pacific Railway bought the El Paso & Southwestern and took over all the track in town and the lines running to it, 1,200 miles in all. Dawson thus became a major coal supplier for the SP, as it was for a few other railroads.

In Dawson, however, bad news always seemed to follow good. During the mid-1920s, Phelps Dodge remodeled its Arizona copper smelters at Douglas and Clifton and replaced coke furnaces with oil-burning ones. Though the *Dawson News* tried to remain upbeat about the changeover— "COPPER OUTLOOK BETTER THAN IN YEARS PAST" proclaimed a 1926 headline—Stag Cañon shut down almost 500 of its coke ovens later that year. The following year, J. B. Morrow, the general outside superintendent who had come to Dawson to manage the coke ovens in 1908, left to take a job with a Pittsburgh, Pennsylvania, coal company. Morrow, a tall, handsome Canadian, had been a well-known figure in town for almost two decades, and his departure surely served as a tangible sign of Dawson's downturn.

Hopes soared when the New Mexico Power Company contracted to supply power to the town and mines in 1927. But when the Rock Island Railroad converted to oil-burning locomotives in 1928, Dawson lost another customer. Phelps Dodge introduced back-saving, mechanical coal loading devices to Stag Cañon in 1928. That same year, Loreta, a Dawson suburb that had flourished from the earliest days, complete with its own school, business district, and rows of neatly kept homes, was abandoned. Mines closed every few months now, and in 1928 and 1929, almost 20 percent of the labor force or 211 were laid off.

The Great Crash of 1929 caused Dawson's coal production to fall 72 percent during the next four years. The *Dawson News* stopped publishing in 1929 and, in 1930, the mighty Welfare Department, managed by the indominitable P. K. Carson, ceased to exist. Carson took over as town supervisor until he was eventually transferred to Arizona. Of the eight mines running in 1929, only four were going by 1930. Stag Cañon instituted four-day and sometimes even two-day work weeks that caused some families to subsist entirely on tortillas and beans. When the Dawson Bank shut its doors for good in 1931, the *Raton Range* said, "It closed not for a lack of business but because of the decline in the town of Dawson."

As strong as the signs of decay were, Dawsonites continued to bank on a turnaround. Young men who left town to join the Civilian Conservation Corps told friends they would be back when jobs reopened. But those jobs never did reappear. In 1932, mines Number One and Two, the town's first two pits as well as the sites of the two great explosions, closed down. Only 300 men now worked in Dawson.

With only one mine open from 1933 on, coal production during the first five years of the 1930s leveled off at about 200,000 tons per year, down from 1.5 million tons per year during the town's heyday. Still more signs of decline became evident: in 1939, the neighboring coal town of Gardiner, New Mexico, closed after almost three decades of activity. Two years later, another nearby mining town, Sugarite, shut down.

A flurry of coal production during World War II gave Dawson an economic boost, but at the same time the war seemed to truly signal the end. After 1946, Dawson's swimming pool never again held water. Bill Saul, the town dentist, commuted from Raton only one day per week. The Mercantile became a self-service store. Orazio and Ferminia Primaveri, owners of a boardinghouse and saloon for as long as anyone in Dawson could remember, relocated to Albuquerque. Another town fixture, electrician and raconteur Terence Scanlon, moved to Raton in 1947 after being fired.

Mine strikes in 1948 and 1949 didn't help things, nor did the crippling forty-day walkout in early 1950. Collection agents turned up in Dawson to repossess cars whose payments miners

Display ad in the Raton Range.

hadn't made. The union's local, proud of its new muscles, flexed for still more demands. When the Stag Cañon Branch wanted to raise medical costs from $3.00 a month to $4.00, a strike resulted. "If you harass somebody all the time, like the union did P.D.," says Charlie Mataya, "they're going to get teed off. I was a union man, but I wasn't fond of that union. I think the union was in part responsible for closing the SOB. If the union would have tried to get along better, Dawson would have stayed open longer."

"Labor didn't close Dawson," argues Margarito Martínez. "It wasn't the local that called all those strikes; it was the national. Labor relations were good between the local and the company; we were in the middle of a three-year contract. We didn't press for that many silly things. We didn't press for a bathhouse, for instance, as they did in other coal camps. Phelps Dodge didn't fight us. The company wanted to raise the price of coal for home fuel from $1.88 a month a ton, to $3.00. The local said no, and the company agreed."

Dawson miners in the late 1940s were making $24.95 a day, almost $10.00 more than ordinary miners elsewhere, and yet coal still rose in price nationwide. Colfax County residents, in fact, were finding other fuels less expensive to heat their homes. Labor problems—the UMWA won a resounding new contract as a result of that 1950 strike—and escalating costs may have speeded Dawson's death, but they didn't by themselves cause it.

Simply, coal had bottomed out. By the end of World War II, coal supplied only about 34 percent of the nation's energy needs, where it had once supplied 85 percent. Natural gas and oil were now in demand. Dieselization of railroads also figured prominently in Dawson's demise. In 1949, the Southern Pacific, which now represented 90 percent of Dawson's income, made plans to abandon its last twenty-five coal-burning locomotives. And, in early 1950, faced with a possible fuel shortage due to a strike, the SP decided it no longer wanted to spend money to stockpile coal at Stag Cañon.

Because the announcement of Dawson's closing had come during a paralyzing coal strike, some people, including members of the media, blamed John L. Lewis, the UMWA president, for the termination of the town. The *Washington Daily News* even offered this editorial ditty:

> Dawson's market is gone
> Soon Dawson will be gone
> For better or for worse
> Take a bow, John L.

Lewis did not deserve blame, for he had nothing to do with coal's decline in this country. Coal towns, in fact, were dying all across the United States. "A blight on the American scene," the *Christian Science Monitor* called them in 1949. More signs: Dawson's neighbor Van Houten, New Mexico, went out of business in 1949; Brilliant, New Mexico, expired soon after; and Koehler a few years later. All those company towns supplied coal to the Santa Fe Railway, which also was going diesel. Down the road a piece from Dawson, Madrid, New Mexico, was about to call it quits, and the coal mines in Gallup also were scaling down. Coal is a "sick industry," said President Harry Truman in 1950.

Dawson's final fight for life was further hurt because Mine Number Six, the lone pit left, sat almost three miles from the tipple, an impractical distance, experts believed. Others felt Number Six was getting too steep, and thus no longer easy to excavate. Perhaps the biggest sign of all came in 1949 when Phelps Dodge sent the chief of its mining division to the town.

"His name was Harry Lavender," says Bill Hancock, who had lived in Dawson all his life. "He came over from Bisbee, and you knew something was up because Lavender was a copper man. He didn't respect coal at all. Right away Lavender got crossways with the union. The miners wanted to go to football and basketball games, and Lavender didn't want that. He couldn't understand that. Harry Lavender, he came to Dawson to be, well, I guess you'd say the 'hatchet man.' After a while, nobody wanted him around. He did his business in Colfax. Nobody liked that man at all."

If signs of sinking had been there long before Harry Lavender's arrival, why had Phelps Dodge kept the town going for so long? Why had the company run only one mine for more than seventeen years? The simple answer is that mechanical equipment had already been installed in the mine, and coal was still needed. But Dawson's singular vitality, the unity that existed there as nowhere else, even in the worst of times, had always earned great respect from Phelps Dodge. With grudging pride perhaps, P.D. refused to close the town until it was no longer feasible in any way to keep it open. The move to terminate wasn't done for financial reasons. By 1950, the company possessed assets of $106 million. Rather, P.D. was a copper company now, and ultimately it decided it wanted no part of coal.

A year after Dawson closed, the town continued to draw breath. Charlie Mataya now salvaged for National Iron and Metal Company. John Krannawitter ran what was left of the dilapidated railroad depot. Herb Mitchell served workmen food and drink at the Snake. Fred Bergamo went from being a miner to driving a bus for the half-dozen or so Dawson kids who went to school in Raton. And Pat Rainwater was still on the job at the power plant. Rainwater liked the peace of

"The Last Hurrah"—April 28, 1950.

deserted Dawson: "There was a group of about ten to twelve families who worked at the power plant and the ranch, and we lived together on Church Row. We'd play cards and go coon hunting and go to Raton. We even gutted the inside of the Community Church and put in some basketball goals there and had games. It was kinda lonesome, but it was nice."

The power plant had been scheduled to shut down about mid-1951, or when all the coal on the ground was depleted. But the plant stayed open, and operated on coal from Koehler. Meanwhile, all around it lay bare foundations. Almost all the mining equipment had vanished—much of it sold to firms in South America, South Africa, or Europe. The washery went to Harlan, Kentucky. By late 1951, Southern Pacific had closed the depot, and crews began tearing up the old Dawson Railway and the tracks to French. Area ranchers, arguing they needed a rail line to ship cattle, successfully fought to keep the Polly, the little spur that went from French to Tucumcari, open. It continued to make its three trips per week until 1962. By 1953, the Oblates of Mary Immaculate, the religious order that served Dawson's Catholic church and other northeastern New Mexico parishes, had left the state. In 1954, when a large power plant opened in Algodones, New Mexico, near Albuquerque, Dawson's plant was disassembled and sold.

For almost twenty years after the closing, Phelps Dodge used the town site solely to run cattle belonging to the company's Diamond D Ranch. During that period, the town itself disappeared from most road atlases. Expectations of a rebirth came in the 1960s when Kaiser Steel considered removing coal from Dawson for its big mill in Fontana, California. But Kaiser passed over the town and in 1966 opened a large underground mine eighteen miles to the north. York Canyon sat on the same vein of coal as Dawson, and followed almost the same rail line as the SP did to French, but no town was built. Instead, employees drove back and forth to York Canyon from Raton, Maxwell, or Cimarron. In 1989, the Pittsburgh & Midway Coal Mining Company purchased the York Canyon mines. Once more, big diesel trains pulled loads right past Dawson and eventually to a power plant in Milwaukee, Wisconsin, which found a need for the coal's low sulphur content. A $1 billion, fifteen-year contract with Pittsburgh & Midway considerably improved Colfax County's economy.

Phelps Dodge shut down its Dawson ranch in 1968, and the following year the company invited the CS Ranch of Cimarron to lease the land for grazing and elk hunting. Founded in 1873 by Frank Springer, one of J. B. Dawson's contemporaries, the CS Ranch became a protective caretaker of the Dawson property. Les Davis, Springer's great-nephew, and owner of the CS, took a particular interest in the vacant town. Davis grew up nearby, and he had fond memories of riding over on horseback to Dawson and buying a double scoop at the Sweet Shop. "We keep Dawson as it is," Davis says, "by locking the gate and watching it."

There are two ways a Dawsonite can get past that gate. One method involves nothing more than remembering, often through the means of a souvenir. These keepsakes can be things as simple as the piece of coal that Steve Schulte took with him in the final days. Numerous Dawsonites remember the town by the roof that covers their heads. "This house belonged to Albino Capone," says Kelly Mora of his rather ordinary looking frame home on Raton's South Thirteenth Street. "His wife was killed on the railroad tracks in Dawson, so we got it. Our original Dawson house is in Cimarron, I think. This was a four-room house when we had it moved to Raton in 1950. It cost us $200 to move it here on a big truck. We paid $400 for the house and $200 to move it here. It cost $75 to cross the railroad tracks here, so I guess the total was $675. A lot of the houses on this street are Dawson houses. You can't recognize many of them, because they've been remodeled so much. This house now has eight rooms."

Fred and Mary Bergamo's remodeled Dawson house in Ute Park, New Mexico, was never a house but, rather, Louis Vitale's barbershop. When Jack and Ona Randall left Dawson, they didn't take a house with them but instead took lumber that Jack had helped tear off other houses. With that wood they built a house in Raton. "We lived there a long time," says Ona, "but it never was really our home. Dawson was our home." Celso Chávez didn't take a house with him when Dawson closed—he took the Dawson Golf Club's clubhouse, site of the celebrated "Last Hurrah" party. Chávez uses it as a summer cabin in Ute Park.

Jeanette O'Belmito saved nothing. After she settled with her mother in an apartment in Temple City, California, Jeanette went right to work down the street—behind a counter again, at a neighborhood drugstore. Always faithful to her employer, Jeanette stayed at that job twelve years, and has been in the same apartment since she moved to California in 1950. "I'm one of those people who don't like to move much," she admits. And yet, she has left California a couple of times to return to New Mexico for Dawson picnics.

A town picnic is the other way a Dawsonite can legally enter the locked gate. The first picnic was held in 1921, at Brookside Park in Pasadena, California, and similar gatherings followed in southern California, where many Dawsonites had relocated. After the town closed, the need for a reunion in New Mexico

Every two years, the Dawson Picnic brings old friends together.

became evident. Early ones were held at Albuquerque's Roosevelt Park, at Alameda, at Sandia Pueblo, and at a campground in the Sandia Mountains. Though Dawsonites appreciated these times together, many wished the affairs could take place at the town site, behind the locked gate. "There's something about those hills around Dawson," says Josephine Valdez Trujillo. "They make you happy to see them again." In time, the picnics got closer to that gate, but even gatherings at Sugarite Canyon, near Raton, lacked something special. Finally, in 1980, Les Davis, with Phelps Dodge's approval, opened Dawson for a picnic. Every two years since, during the Labor Day weekend, Davis has unlocked the gate. In 1992, the Dawson Picnic Committee, grateful for Davis's cooperation, honored him with a plaque.

The picnics, which have drawn as many as 2,000 people from across the United States, are meant to be a continuation of the town's Field Days, started by Phelps Dodge in the 1920s. Held now on a shaded, open spot south of where the Dawson Hotel stood, and north of the old filling station, the picnics feature no athletic contests or first-aid competition as they once did. Still, many of the same people—and at least half a dozen nationalities—attend these modern-day parties. There, for instance, is Celso Chávez, quietly reminiscing in a folding chair. Marcia McClary Beall is there, too, meeting for the first time in years one of her high school teachers. All sorts of extended families—granddaughters, great-grandsons, and distant cousins, who never lived an hour in the town—show up at the Dawson Picnic, many arriving in motor homes. There is barbecuing and talking, but mostly the latter: about a long-ago football game, or the time someone set off firecrackers beneath Mr. Fenlon's porch, or how life was so hard that mothers used to put kids to bed in the afternoon so they could wash their one set of clothes. When the talk runs out, which takes awhile, people poke about the place that lies beneath two lonely smokestacks and the bones of 100 coke ovens. Picnickers hunt among the crowd for a neighbor or for the spot where their house used to stand. Some drive one and a half miles up to Loreta, where they find only mounds of dirt; others hike up Capitan to discover a pile of rubble. Some guests study the names and dates at the town cemetery or peer into the empty swimming pool. Some scavenge for chunks of slag or bricks, while others use metal detectors to search for a single nail.

Bear hugs and tears dominate a Dawson Picnic. ''It's like coming home to heaven,'' says Nick Di Domenico. One year Charles Buttram wandered around the town with his son and grandson. At the spot of his boyhood home, the senior Buttram pointed to a big cottonwood still standing in what used to be his front yard. That tree, Buttram told his family, was where his grandfather, Jacob Buttram, used to tie him up as a boy so the old man could keep an eye on him. Buttram had the younger men stand in front of the tree while he pulled out a camera to record the memory. The family already had some idea of how fond Charlie Buttram was of Dawson. His grandson, a high school student, is named Michael Dawson Buttram.

What brings so many back? ''A common bond of having shared something,'' says Eleen Bailey Owen. ''A real depth of kinship that goes far beyond a high school or college re-union.'' ''A sense of security,'' says Nick Gonzáles. ''You come back looking for that, but you really don't find it. See, there'll never be a place like Dawson, a place without discrimination, with great friendliness, with everybody helping each other. There'll never be a place like that again, but you can still remember.''

Not everybody wants to remember, particularly the hard times or the limitations. Jeanette O'Belmito is one of those people. ''Dawson was a small town, and there was always criticism. If you sat on the porch, people talked about why. If you went inside, people talked about why.'' Terence Scanlon, who loved Dawson and worked there for more than thirty years, never went to a picnic before he died in 1965 at age seventy-nine. ''There was always a little bitterness about losing his job,'' says his son Jerry. ''P.D. was a father figure, but at other times the company kept you under its thumb.'' All the other Scanlons, several generations worth, in fact, do go to the picnics. ''Dad used to say that nothing was as bad as it seems,'' says Jerry. ''We've tried to remember that.''

Dawson today: in the hearts and minds of many, it still exists.

A Dawson Picnic concludes perhaps like no other get-together. "At the end," says Nick Di Domenico, "nobody says good-bye. You just leave." Indeed, it's as if saying those parting words carried a finality, for no one fails to notice that every two years the number of true Dawsonites gets smaller.

Though no one has been buried in the Dawson Cemetery since the town closed, for years afterward no one took care of it either. On occasion a Dawsonite would come by and put flowers on a grave, but the general deterioration of the place only grew worse. Weeds smothered the ground, *cercados,* or little fences, that surrounded some graves fell over, markers rusted and toppled. The eyesore greatly disturbed Les Davis. "Those miners," he told people, "they gave their lives to Phelps Dodge, just as soldiers did to the wars in this country. It should look like Arlington Cemetery." Kelly Mora also was concerned. "My wife's family is there, and when we would go see it it would bother me. Why, cattle were even going over the place." As a member of the New Mexico Legislature, Mora began to pressure Phelps Dodge for help. Meanwhile, the company had already heard from Davis about the cemetery. Eventually, P.D. authorized and funded repairs to the road leading to the grave site and to the fence that surrounds it. In 1991, the New Mexico Legislature issued a proclamation of gratitude to Phelps Dodge. The following year, the Dawson Cemetery, with 630 marked graves, appeared on the National Register of Historic Places, the first and so far only cemetery in the state to be listed. The memorial came about through the work of Corinne Sze of the Historic Preservation Division of the Of-fice of Cultural Affairs in Santa Fe. "It means," says Sze, "that governmental organizations can't bulldoze it."

The cemetery may be safe, but the town's future is unknown. Dawson's 50,285 deeded acres have been on the market since the mid-1980s, and more than 100 interested buyers have looked at the property. "We're not motivated to sell," explains Ken Bennett, P.D.'s director of real estate development in Phoenix. Though Phelps Dodge did open a copper smelter in Hidalgo County in 1980, and did experiment with crushed coal to fuel it, the company has no plans to get back into coal mining, even though Dawson has approximately another fifty years' worth of coal left in it.

What Dawson also has is quality land that's never been strip-mined. Grazing land comprises about 20,000 acres. Another 20,000 acres features ponderosa and other timber. Plus, there are irrigation rights on the Vermejo River. According to Bennett, the property also shows some oil and gas. Who might be a prospective buyer? "Probably a gentleman rancher tied with hunting," says Bennett. "A power plant is a possibility. One man wanted to put a thoroughbred quarter horse ranch on the place. A good mix might be recreation and mineral production." No one can say what would happen to the Dawson Picnic if the property is sold, but three times Phelps Dodge has come "very close" to making a deal. Oh, yes, the cost. Eighteen million dollars, or about 5,000 times what John Barkley Dawson paid for his "hand of God." If the figure sounds high, just run it by a Dawsonite. More than likely he'll tell you it's a bargain.

BIBLIOGRAPHY

BOOKS:

Allen, James B. *The Company Town in the American West.* Norman: University of Oklahoma Press, 1966.

Armstrong, Ruth W. *The Chases of Cimarron.* Albuquerque: New Mexico Stockman, 1981.

Cleland, Robert Glass. *A History of Phelps Dodge, 1834-1950.* New York: Alfred A. Knopf, 1952.

Crocchiola, Fr. Stanley Francis. *The Dawson Story.* Pantex, Tex.: F. Stanley, 1961.

Crocchiola, Fr. Stanley Francis. *The Dawson Tragedies.* Pep, Tex.: F. Stanley, 1964.

Davis, Ellis Arthur, ed. *The Historical Encyclopedia of New Mexico.* Albuquerque: New Mexico Historical Society, 1945.

Hammond, George P. *Rediscovery of New Mexico.* Albuquerque: University of New Mexico Press, 1966.

Jenkins, Myra Ellen and Albert H. Schroeder. *A Brief History of New Mexico.* Albuquerque: University of New Mexico Press, 1974.

Jenkinson, Michael. *Ghost Towns of New Mexico: Playthings of the Wind.* Albuquerque: University of New Mexico Press, 1967.

Kahn, Kathy. *Fruits of Our Labor.* New York: G. P. Putnam's Sons, 1982.

Keleher, William A. *Maxwell Land Grant, a New Mexico Item.* Santa Fe: Rydal Press, 1942.

Kern, Robert. *Labor in New Mexico: Unions, Strikes and Social History Since 1881.* Albuquerque: University of New Mexico Press, 1983.

Kingsolver, Barbara. *Holding the Line.* Ithaca, N.Y.: ILP Press, 1989.

Koehler, A. E., Jr. *New Mexico, The Land of Opportunity.* Albuquerque: Albuquerque Morning Journal, 1915.

Looney, Ralph. *Haunted Highways: The Ghost Towns of New Mexico.* Albuquerque: University of New Mexico Press, 1983.

Myrick, David F. *New Mexico's Railroads.* Albuquerque: University of New Mexico Press, 1990.

Papanikolas, Zeese. *Buried Unsung: Louis Tiklas and the Ludlow Massacre.* Salt Lake City: University of Utah Press, 1982.

Pearson, Jim Berry. *The Maxwell Land Grant.* Norman: University of Oklahoma Press, 1961.

Van Kleeck, Mary. *Mines and Management.* New York: Russell Sage Foundation, 1934.

Vecsey, George. *One Sunset a Week: The Story of a Coal Miner.* New York: Saturday Review Press/E. P. Dutton, 1974.

Williams, Stephen K. *Cases Argued and Decided in the Supreme Court of the United States.* Book 38, Lawyers Edition. New York: The Lawyers Cooperative Publishing Co., 1926.

Wilson, Delphine Dawson. *John Barkley Dawson, 1830-1918.* San Diego: Delphine Dawson Wilson, 1975.

ARTICLES:

Becchetti, Fred. "Home Again to Dawson." *Raton Range* (Special Supplement) 107, no. 68, (2 September 1988): 1-8.

Davis, Stephanie. "Only the Ghosts Left at Dawson—Coal Camp of the World." *Sangre de Cristo Chronicle* 14, no. 24 (16 June 1988): 8-10.

"Dawson Cemetery Placed on National Register." *New Mexico Preservation* 10, no. 1 (Summer 1993): 1, 4-7.

"Dawson Fueled Arizona Mines and Smelters." *Paydirt,* Phelps Dodge Centennial 1881-1981 (Summer 1981): 116-121.

Hanson, Murray. "Every Single Soul Left Town." *Coal People* 5, no. 1 (May 1980): 36-39.

Hoffman, Gretchen K. "Coal Geology and Mining History in the Dawson Area, Southeastern Raton Coal Field, New Mexico." *New Mexico Geological Society Guidebook,* 41st Field Conference (1990): 397-403.

Melzer, Richard. "A Death in Dawson: The Demise of a Southwestern Company Town." *New Mexico Historical Review* 55, no. 4 (October 1980): 309-330.

Melzer, Richard. "Welfare Capitalism in a New Mexico Camp, Dawson, 1920-1929." *Southwest Economy & Society* 6, no. 1 (Fall 1982): 12-34.

Price, Jess and E. A. Scholer. "Disaster by the Decade." *True West* (May 1985): 34-40.

Sheridan, Jo E. "Coal Mines and Plant of Stag Cañon Fuel Co." *The Mining World* (31 July 1909): 271-278.

Tidwell, Dewey. "Dawson: A Personal Recollection." *New Mexico Magazine* 59, no. 6 (June 1981): 53-59.

Woods, Betty. "Trip of the Month—Dawson." *New Mexico Magazine* 42, no. 1 (January 1964): 35.

SPECIAL PUBLICATIONS, UNPUBLISHED MANUSCRIPTS, DOCUMENTS, AND MISCELLANEOUS:

Cale, Jo C. *Ghosts of New Mexico,* videotape distributed by Armchair Entertainment, Albuquerque, New Mexico, 1992.

Carson, Paul K. "A History of Dawson." Dawson, New Mexico, 1940.

Covert, Enes Federici Caraglio. *Dawson, the Town That Was: A Family Story.* Albuquerque, New Mexico, 1984.

Craig, Carlos J. "The Unionization of the Mines in Dawson, New Mexico." Master's thesis, Highlands University, Las Vegas, New Mexico, 1970.

Dawson. Home movie produced by Hubert Loy, 1938-1939.

Dawson. Promotional film produced by Phelps Dodge Corporation, 1917.

Ford, Dan. *The History of New Mexico High School Football.* Bayfield, Colorado, 1980.

Fox, Maier B. *United We Stand: A History of the United Mine Workers of America.* Washington, D.C., 1990.

"Mine Inspector for the Territory of New Mexico," 1903-1911.

Miner's Pick, Dawson High School newspaper, 5 May 1950.

"Oblates in the Land of Enchantment." *Province Newsletter.* Missionary Oblates of Mary Immaculate (September-October, 1990).

Phelps Dodge Annual Report, 1909-1950.

"Report of the State Mine Inspector of New Mexico," 1912-1928.

Robertson, Andrew G. "Labor and Equity: A Look at Life, Labor, and the Mines of Dawson, New Mexico." Senior thesis, The College of Wooster, Wooster, Ohio, 1979.

Secrest, Donald G. "The Dawson Story." Taos, New Mexico, 1950.

Shelton, J. T. (Ted) "Reminiscence of a Grandiose Town: Personal and Factual Information about Dawson, New Mexico, and Phelps Dodge Corporation Stag Cañon Branch." Ajo, Arizona, July 1976.

Skandale, Elizabeth. "A Mine Explosion." La Cañada, California, 1977.

Wilson, Delphine Dawson. *The John Barkley Dawson Family.* Springer, New Mexico, 1983.

Ye Coke Breeze, Dawson High School yearbook, 1921.

NEWSPAPERS:

(*Note:* From 1900 to 1950, the Raton newspaper was known variously as the *Raton Daily Range* and the *Raton Range.*)

Albuquerque Journal
Albuquerque Tribune
Christian Science Monitor
Cimarron Legend
Cimarron News
Clovis News Journal
Dawson News
Denver Post
Enchantment
New York Times
Raton Daily Range
Raton Range
Roy Record
Sangre de Cristo Chronicle
Santa Fe New Mexican
Santa Fe Register

Santa Fe Reporter
Springer Times
Taos News

Trinidad Chronicle News
Tucumcari Daily News

OTHER SOURCES:

Archdiocese of Santa Fe: Belinda Sánchez

Arthur Johnson Memorial Library, Raton: Richard Azar, Betty Lloyd

Menaul Historical Library, Albuquerque

Museum of New Mexico, Santa Fe: Arthur Olivas, Orlando Romero

New Mexico Activities Association: John Daniel

New Mexico Bureau of Mines & Mineral Resources, Socorro: Bob Eveleths, Gretchen K. Hoffman

New Mexico State Library, Santa Fe: Betty Sena

New Mexico State Records Center & Archives, Santa Fe: Ron Montoya

New Mexico State University Library, Las Cruces: Austin Hoover

Phelps Dodge Corporation, Phoenix: Ken Bennett, Lucy Diana, Kim Sterling, William C. Tubman

Raton Museum: Tomás Burch, Mike Palomino

University of New Mexico: David King Dunaway; Richard Melzer (Valencia Campus); Joseph McKenzie, Zimmerman Library; Center for Southwest Research

Oblates of Mary Immaculate, San Antonio, Texas: Gladys Novak

Presbyterian Historical Society, Philadelphia

United Mine Workers of America, Washington, D.C.

Also: Ed Beaumont, Jim Boggio, Pedro Calderón, Chuck Ferris, Bern Gantner, Eleanor Hampson, Jim Hulsman, Mike Pappas, Nancy Robertson, Marc Simmons

AUTHOR INTERVIEWS

from February 1992 through April 1993

Andazola, Josephine
Arellano, Tony
Beall, Marcia McClary
Bennett, Ken
Bergamo, Bruno
Bergamo, Doris Dahl
Bergamo, Fred
Bergamo, Mary Rubino
Black, Harmon
Brannon, Leroy
Brannon, Lulamay
Britton, Grayce Padilla
Brown, Anita M. Flood
Brozovich, Paul
Brozovich, Ruth
Buttram, Charles
Buttram, Lorraine Calderelli
Carlini, Ernest
Cericola, Fred
Chávez, Celso
Christie, Tillie Zauhar
Cimino, Fr. Michael
Córdova, Dave
Crocchiola, Fr. Stanley
Dahl, Ed
Dale, George
Dale, Katherine McCarty
Davis, Les
Dazzo, Gertrude Donnelly
Dazzo, Nicholas

Di Domenico, Margie Bergamo
Di Domenico, Nick
DiLorenzo, Arthur
DiLorenzo, Margaret Mary Beall
Faba, Mike
Faba, Sabina DiLorenzo Cericola
Federici, Judge William
Forte, Lena Colaizzi
García, Amelia
García, José Marcos
Gonzáles, Nick
Hancock, Bill
Hancock, Janet Wilson
Harbin, Patricia Smith
Herrera, Emogene Chase
Herrera, Juan
Hoffman, Cecilia Lucero
Holdridge, Diane Pool
Howard, Alice DiLorenzo
Kinney, Bruce
Kinney, Harry
Kinney, Isabel
Lancieri, John
Lopez, Julio
Lucero, Anna Zauhar
Lucero, Arthur
Lucero, Robert
Mares, Ernest
Martínez, Longino

Martínez, Margarito
Mataya, Charles
McClary, Alberta
McClary, Robert
McIntyre, Emily Palumbo
Miller, Sylvia Peppin York
Mora, Kelly
Mora, Livia
Muench, Cicily Smith
Myers, Carol McClary
Myers, Dwight
O'Belmito Jeanette
Owen, Eleen Bailey
Pacheco, Perfecto
Pool, Hazel
Ponce, Jess
Ragni, Jay
Rainwater, Pat
Randall, Ona
Reza, Henry
Reza, Mary Frances García
Rivera, Albert
Sackett, Mary Alice Secrest
Salvo, Sam
Saracino, Virgil
Saul, Hazel
Saul, Dr. William
Scanlon, Gene
Scanlon, Jerry

Scanlon, Jim
Scanlon, Pat
Scanlon, Roger
Schulte, Al
Schulte, Steve
Sekot, Anita Valdez
Sekot, John
Shelton, Ruth
Shipe, Lucille Hubbard
Skandale, George
Sluga, Hester
Sluga, Joe
Stratton, Laura Palumbo
Sze, Corinne
Tozzie, Viallie
Trani, Domenic
Trujillo, Abraham
Trujillo, Gabe
Trujillo, Josephine Valdez
Trujillo, Louise Primaveri
Trujillo, Pete
Viramontes, Concepción
Viramontes, Isabel, Martínez
Whiteley, Bill
Wiggins, Vernice Smock
Wilson, Delphine Dawson
Wilson, Don
Wilson, Sara Palumbo
Wilson, Shirley Bain